CISTERCIAN STUDIES SERIES: NU

M000229995

Bernadette McNary-Zak

Useful Servanthood

CISTERCIAN STUDIES SERIES: NUMBER TWO HUNDRED TWENTY-FOUR

Useful Servanthood

A Study of Spiritual Formation in the Writings of Abba Ammonas

Bernadette McNary-Zak

With the Greek corpus of Ammonas in English translation
by Nada Conic, Lawrence Morey, OCSO,
and Richard Upsher Smith, Jr.

α

Cistercian Publications
www.cistercianpublications.org

LITURGICAL PRESS
Collegeville, Minnesota
www.litpress.org

A Cistercian Publications title published by Liturgical Press

Cistercian Publications
Editorial Offices
Abbey of Gethsemani
3642 Monks Road
Trappist, Kentucky 40051
www.cistercianpublications.org

1   2   3   4   5   6   7   8   9

Library of Congress Cataloging-in-Publication Data

McNary-Zak, Bernadette.
    Useful servanthood : a study of spiritual formation in the writings of Abba Ammonas / Bernadette McNary-Zak ; with the Greek corpus of Ammonas in English translation by Nada Conic, Lawrence Morey, and Richard Upsher Smith.
       p.   cm. — (Cistercian studies series ; no. 224)
    Includes bibliographical references.
    ISBN 978-0-87907-224-7 — ISBN 978-0-87907-922-2 (e-book)
    1. Ammonas, Saint, 4th cent.   2. Spiritual formation.   I. Conic, Nada.
II. Morey, Lawrence.   III. Smith, Richard Upsher.   IV. Ammonas, Saint,
4th cent. Selections. English   V. Title.   VI. Series.

BR65.A3276M36   2010
248.8'94—dc22   2010020560

Contents

Preface   vii

Part One
Understanding the Writings of Abba Ammonas

CHAPTER ONE
An Introduction to the Literature of the Desert   3

CHAPTER TWO
The Correspondence of Abba Ammonas   15

CHAPTER THREE
The Monastic Journey   33

CHAPTER FOUR
The Gift of Discernment   64

CHAPTER FIVE
A Community of Discernment   85

EPILOGUE
Monasticism, Mysticism, and *Ecclesia*   109

Part Two
The Writings of Abba Ammonas

Letters   114

Instructions   139

Exhortations, or Paragraphs of Encouragement   155

Select Bibliography   167

Preface

A brother asked Abba Ammonas, "Give me a word," and the old man replied, "Go make your thoughts like those of the evildoers who are in prison. For they are always asking when the magistrate will come, awaiting him in anxiety. Even so the monk ought to give himself at all times to accusing his own soul, saying, 'Unhappy wretch that I am. How shall I stand before the judgment seat of Christ? What shall I say to him in my defense?' If you give yourself continually to this, you may be saved."[1]

By sharing stories like this one, Egyptian desert monks of the late fourth century preserved a collective memory of one of their best-remembered members, Abba Ammonas. Their primary intention, however, was less biographical than our modern sensibilities might imagine. Rather, their acts of preservation and transmission were shaped by deep convictions regarding the enduring tangibility of Abba Ammonas' presence and the veracity of his words. This saying's ability to capture so compactly the ethos of desert monastic practice through its teasing, compelling sense of transparency, and simplicity, posed a real challenge to its audiences. As in other forms of wisdom literature, much of the potency operative in this saying was found in what lay behind and beyond the words. Indeed, it was the unspoken reality of desert monastic practice that animated the imaginations of Christians of late antiquity and prompted their queries. For many contemporary historians of early Christianity, their questions remain relevant. What was the experience that supplied Abba Ammonas and his fellow monks with a worldview that rested on a radical overturning of commonly perceived notions of happiness and judgment? How and why did Abba Ammonas know that this monk must adopt the same worldview? On what grounds was Abba Ammonas compelled to speak and the monk to listen?

Scholars have long addressed the nature, exercise, and role of spiritual formation in the context of desert monastic practice. This book applies the theoretical contributions of many of these studies to a presentation of the specific model of spiritual formation advanced by Abba Ammonas, a prominent fourth-century monastic leader whose extant writings remain largely unexamined. Given the nature of his monastic ties and the presence of a body of his writings, it remains striking that Abba Ammonas is an underrepresented figure in our study of early Christian monasticism. An examination of Abba Ammonas' writings illumines how discernment, a spiritual gift pervasive in early monastic circles, was discussed and cultivated in a local context and so provides another lens for considering the relationship between mystical experience and monastic practice in the life of the early Christian community.

The book falls into two parts. The first part situates Abba Ammonas in his historical and theological contexts. It begins with a brief discussion of the nature of spiritual guidance in fourth-century Egyptian desert monastic practice in order to locate Abba Ammonas' *Letters, Instructions,* and *Exhortations* and then proceeds to a systematic reconstruction of the model of spiritual formation found in these works. This is followed by a consideration of the contribution this model made in the contexts of Abba Ammonas' monastic network and the local church community.

The second part of the book contains English translations of Abba Ammonas' *Letters, Instructions,* and *Exhortations* as they survive in Greek. While there are French translations of these works, and an English translation of the Syriac *Letters,* the Greek manuscript tradition remains inaccessible to many readers; the translation of these texts is intended to add to the body of writings available.

Scholarship never takes place in isolation and I am grateful to many for their assistance in the construction of this book. I received gifts of funding and time at several critical periods. In a serendipitous sequence of events, a grant in the summer of 2003 from the Wabash Center for Teaching and Learning in Theology and Religion enabled me to focus attention on writing, and to do so in the context of dialogue and fellowship with colleagues whose contemporary work and lives were centered in one way or another on questions of discernment and community. I am especially grateful to Professor Susan Ashbrook Harvey and Rev. Dr. Paul O. Myhre for their help during this period. Further assistance was received in a course release in the fall 2004 semester through the generosity of a faculty development grant funded by the Andrew W. Mellon Foundation. I am especially grateful to my colleagues in the Religious Studies Department and in the Inter-disciplinary Humanities program at Rhodes College for their support at this time.

Public presentation of much of the scholarship in this book occurred in several forums. Audiences at annual and regional meetings of the American Academy of Religion, the Byzantine Studies Conference, and the International Congress of Medieval Studies in Kalamazoo, Michigan, challenged me to think with greater clarity and helped me to appreciate the value of Abba Ammonas' thought in a broader context. Students in my undergraduate courses, past and present, may recognize some of this material as well; they have been an invaluable audience as they continue to help me to hone my teaching about monastic practice. Dr. E. Rozanne Elder, Fr. Mark Scott, and the anonymous readers at Cistercian Publications provided insightful readings and comments on an earlier version of the manuscript and translations. My mother, Tusa McNary, first drew my attention to the cover image. I am especially grateful to her for the conversations that led to its eventual selection, and to Dr. Russell Hartman and those in the Department of Anthropology at the California Academy of Sciences who made its use possible. Finally, my deepest thanks go to David.

B. M. Z.

Notes

1. Ammonas, *AP* 1, in *The Sayings of the Desert Fathers: The Alphabetical Collection,* trans. Benedicta Ward, Cistercian Studies Series 26 (Kalamazoo: Cistercian Publications, 1975).

Part One

Understanding the Writings of Abba Ammonas

CHAPTER ONE

An Introduction to the Literature of the Desert

Abba Ammonas was asked, "What is the 'narrow and hard way' [Matt 7:14]?" He replied, "The 'narrow and hard way' is this, to control your thoughts, and to strip yourself of your own will, for the sake of God. This is also the meaning of the sentence, 'We have left everything and followed you' [Matt 19:27]."[1]

As this saying records, Abba Ammonas articulates the belief of every monastic storyteller that the monastic practice is a specific form of Christian discipleship. The saying conveys a common depiction of spiritual guidance found among semi-anchoritic desert monks of the fourth century, whereby the monastic amma or abba imparts wisdom and insight to an eager visitor seeking counsel. In their descriptions of these encounters, the *Apophthegmata Patrum* illustrate how the receptivity of such visitors validated as legitimate a recognizable mark of holiness in late antiquity. Many visitors believed that "by departing from the flawed orbit of ordinary men, by waging heroic battle against the demons," desert ammas and abbas "recovered the primeval perfection of Adam that existed before the fall from grace."[2] As Peter Brown observes, desert ammas and abbas "had to work and to be seen to work. Charisma was the visible manifestation of an equally visible ascetic 'labor,' whose rhythms and physical effect were palpable to all."[3] Such palpability was harnessed and contained in the oral and written sayings of these holy men and women. These sayings highlight the activity of spiritual guidance, the "sight and sound, observation and dialogue,"[4] that shaped the relationship between holy persons and their disciples. Benedicta Ward writes that the sayings "are neither accounts of the way of life of the monks nor records of their teaching, but glimpses of them as they are known to their disciples."[5] Although idealized to some extent, the *Apophthegmata Patrum* provides evidence for a mode of teaching and learning about the spiritual life that forms the basis of our discussion.

The Relationship of Spiritual Guidance

As in philosophical and rabbinic circles, teaching and learning were highly personalized activities among the desert monks. Many times learning began with a request, "Give me a word, abba." First and foremost, a disciple's validation of the holiness of a desert amma or abba acknowledged the embodiment of those teachings and practices in Scripture and tradition from which such holiness derived. Texts like the *Apophthegmata Patrum*, the *History of the Monks*, and the *Lives* were explicit in creating spiritual ties between a desert abba or amma, former monastic guides, and prominent biblical predecessors in order to show how their wisdom was founded on Scripture. By preserving this "heritage of power"[6] holy men and women grounded their words and practices in the framework of a tradition of interpretation recognized as holy, necessary, and true by early Christians.

The relationship of teaching and learning among the desert monks was also rooted in claims of a common experience. "No one could set himself up as a mere oracle of wisdom, but was expected to reflect in his own life the fruits of a vigorous and enduring regime of self-perfection."[7] Like his disciple, the desert abba had accepted a call to pursue the ascetic life and to strive for union with the divine, which brought him into solidarity with his fellow monks. The "ethical responsibilities associated with speaking and hearing were believed to have a profound effect on one's capacity to interpret the words of Scripture and the words of power uttered by the elders . . . Verbal purity and integrity were felt to be indispensable for engaging in meaningful interpretation."[8] These dimensions are illumined well in a saying that recounts one of Abba Ammonas' visits to Abba Antony. According to this saying, after watching Abba Ammonas beat a stone at his request, Abba Antony is said to have declared, "'Has this stone said anything?' Abba Ammonas replied, 'No.' Then Antony said, 'You too will be able to do that,' and that is what happened. Abba Ammonas advanced to the point where his goodness was so great he took no notice of wickedness."[9]

For many desert monks, teaching and learning required sustained oversight. This required geographic proximity and longer acquaintance with a desert abba. Graham Gould writes that teaching "takes place in the context of a personal relationship, which makes great demands on both parties involved."[10] The process of learning required "self-disclosure, endurance, and obedience" on the part of the disciple.[11] Richard Valantasis has observed that teaching entailed training "the disciple in a way of perceiving and relating to the mental and emotional self, the religious community, and the wider world. The substance of the training revolved about the transmission of traditional material regarding the interior life."[12] Desert ammas and abbas often tailored their teaching to the specific needs of their disciples. For their part, the disciples were convinced that their elders were "able to identify and describe their personal problems, and to propose for them suitable solutions."[13] On occasion, such specificity would have required the desert amma or abba to incorporate local imagery and personal experience into a teaching. So, for an audience whose lives were dependent on the behavior of the Nile River, Abba Ammonas' analogy describing the reception of lasting spiritual gifts from the Holy Spirit would have had a highly specific meaning: "For as with a ship when the wind is fair, her twin rudders are driven more and so she travels a great distance, and so also the sailors rejoice and are at ease, so is the second fervor, bringing calm in every way."[14]

For the desert amma or abba the relationship with a disciple was a means of "testing [one's] own endurance, submission, and integrity in teaching by example and by personal involvement with a disciple's problems and temptations."[15] In this way, teaching was a product of and a contributor to the interior formation of these holy men and women. Visitors and disciples believed that these spiritual guides had acquired that inner purity of heart possible in the monastic life and had been given the gift of discernment. Discernment was the distinguishing feature that separated the desert amma or abba from the disciple: it was precisely through the attainment of discernment that the desert amma or abba was able to serve and to be recognized. "This supposed inspiration by God was the essential basis of trust in the teaching of the fathers. An apparently intimate relationship with God, a complete dependence upon him, did more than anything else to give experienced ascetics a permanent standing in the eyes of other men."[16] Discernment was also foundational to the process of spiritual formation. As William Harmless observes: "if a 'word of salvation' was a key specially fit to open a particular monk's heart, then the abba's ability to speak that word implied astute discernment."[17]

The centrality of discernment attests to the belief among the desert monks that the relationship between desert ammas and abbas and their disciples was "seen as a form of training through obedience on which a disciple's attainment of the virtues and qualities which are the aim of the monastic life was directly dependent—and which directly affects his standing before God as well."[18] It was "the word of Christ and his example, seen in the light of the Holy Spirit" that "formed the guiding force" of teaching and learning among the desert monks.[19] Hardly ends in themselves, teaching and learning were born of a divine call and so were consecrated, commissioned acts with the power to transform teacher and disciple. That is to say, desert ammas and abbas and their disciples shared a vocation that was "pre-eminently an imitation of Christ."[20] In this context, spiritual guidance was essentially about aiding the disciple in his quest as the divine was always the source of spiritual instruction. Hans J. W. Drijvers observes that in "the hard exercise of his will the holy man gains insight into God's saving thought—asceticism and acquirement of wisdom are two sides of the same *imitatio Christi*—and he displays this insight in his acts of power, which always aim at the salvation of men. The desert is the place of trial and hence preeminently the place for exercising the will: at the same time the desert is between servitude and slavery and the promised land."[21]

It is in this sense that the desert amma's or abba's public exercise of discernment was construed as a manifestation of the activity of the divine. For the desert amma and abba, such perception empowered the capacity for prophecy, what Tomas Spidlik describes as "being able to speak in the name of God."[22] As desert monastic practice drew more public attention in the early decades of the fourth century, acts of intercession on behalf of faithful disciples and others increased accordingly and desert ammas and abbas served many through their exercise of the spiritual gift of discernment. These holy women and men were regarded as viable sources of wisdom, courage, and strength by those who came to the desert from their cities, towns, and villages seeking counsel and mediation. According to the sources from the period the involvement of these holy women and men was far-reaching in form and in content, as they addressed matters practical and esoteric. By way of example, we may consider the papyrus fragment from 324 CE that is evidence for the activity of a deacon, Antoninus, and a monk, Isaac, who intervened on behalf of a man who was being assaulted and later were asked to serve as witnesses to the attack.[23] Likewise, we can turn to the *History of the Monks*, in which we encounter Bes who, at the request of the local farmers, drove a wild hippopotamus from the area by invoking the name of Jesus Christ, and Theon who was said to have spent the greater part of his day healing many by stretching out his hand through the window of his monastic cell.[24]

Among the desert monks, such acts of intercession were often identified as acts of prayer. Indeed, it was in humility and obedience before the divine that Bes and Theon exercised discernment and functioned as intercessors. Yet, it was left to their audiences, those unnamed observers and recipients, to accept their intercession as a means rather than an end. If such acts were, in fact, in accordance with the will of the divine, then intercession might also validate the process of spiritual formation advocated by the particular spiritual guide to whom they were attributed. In a highly visible way acts of intercession might distinguish the desert amma or abba as both a resource and as a marker for the activity of the divine. By identifying false thinking and proposing right thinking, the desert amma or abba could challenge her or his audiences *to see* rightly; by offering prayer on their behalf, the desert amma or abba could challenge them *to be* accordingly. Clearly, the gift of discernment characterized in such acts entailed participation in the activity of the divine through intimate involvement with and engagement in the affairs of the world. Drawing on the writings of the desert fathers, Augustine Roberts, OCSO, writes that monasticism is a reformation, a conversion, for which "the beginning and the end of this conversion process is mystical, namely, the person of Jesus Christ, his way of life and his inner experience as the Son of the Father's Love."[25] For the desert monks, the gift of discernment was connected, then, to this mystical process of conversion.

It is for this reason that, in many regions of the eastern Roman Empire, the exercise of discernment by spiritual mothers and fathers like Abba Ammonas expanded existing concepts of patronage. Certainly, there is evidence that the relations between the desert abba and the local church community created tension between the charismatic authority of the desert monk and the institutional authority of the local bishop.[26] As Timothy D. Barnes concludes, with the rise and reforms under Constantine and his sons, the Christian bishop "possessed an ascribed status, his authority was inherent in his office, and he was at the centre of a web of local patronage. His position thus conferred on him a very real political power."[27] Such power would, at times, conform to and, at times, compete with the popular authority of the desert monk.

As prophetic voices to the Christians of their day, many spiritual mothers and fathers by their renunciation were afforded a perspective for evaluating what they perceived as diluted piety and frivolous excess in their fellow Christians, including their bishops. The correspondence of Abba Ammonas provides a way for us to consider as complementary rather than competing the perspectives on the exercise of discernment as a ministry shared by monk and bishop in several fourth-century Christian communities.

Overview of this Study

The first part of this book situates Abba Ammonas in his historical and theological contexts. Chapter 2 begins with a presentation and assessment of the source material for Abba Ammonas and his model of spiritual formation. The monastic correspondence of Abba Ammonas is one of our primary sources. His *Letters, Instructions,* and *Exhortations* are chronologically placed in "the generation of pioneers," that period during which Egyptian monasticism was exclusively Egyptian.[28] A sizeable number of sayings are attributed to Abba Ammonas and his practice is preserved as well on the pages of the *History of the Monks of Egypt.* These writings are distinct from the extant *Letters, Instructions,* and *Exhortations* in significant ways, yet their inclusion is necessary if we are to understand the impact of Abba Ammonas and of his teachings.

The process of spiritual formation defined by Abba Ammonas in these sources is presented in chapter three. For the purpose of discussion, I have chosen to refer to this process in terms of spiritual formation. While it is certainly plausible that Abba Ammonas would have found this designation foreign or insufficient, I intend its use to highlight the particularity of his vision of the monastic practice. For him, spiritual formation was a process of acquiring and maintaining righteousness. It required purification, a cleansing of the body and of the soul in order to become worthy to receive and retain a divine power. In his role as spiritual father, Abba Ammonas participated in a spiritual lineage of righteous men that included the Old Testament patriarchs, prophets, and Saint Paul. Like them, he sought to create relationships rooted in prayer and in love that cultivated a specific awareness of the presence and authority of the divine as abba and guide. For Abba Ammonas, the abba-disciple relationship was intentionally a heuristic, didactic device for the invisible yet wholly real paradigm of monastic practice: the relation between the monk and the divine. Operative in the abba-disciple relation as Abba Ammonas defined it was an implicit awareness of its ability and of its frailty to serve as a prototype for the relation between the monk as disciple and the divine as master. Because of this Abba Ammonas stressed that spiritual formation be situated in the context of the Christian monastic community, a spirit-centered community of righteousness rooted in love and hospitality in which the divine was both host and guest and into which the monk was invited, through the process of spiritual formation, to participate.

When his model of spiritual formation is examined in the context of his immediate monastic network it is possible to identify the specific emphasis of Ammonian spirituality: the invitation to Christian discipleship and the ability to choose its pursuit through the creation of a hospitable body for prayerful service to the world and mystical union with the divine. According to Abba Ammonas, the reception of divine power was a sign of right relations between the desert monk and the divine and could lead, in turn, to the spiritual gift of discernment and so to a commissioning for service to others. For these desert monks, it was the will of the divine that they return to the world in order to assist others through their exercise of the gift of discernment.

Chapter 4 examines how Abba Ammonas, defined as a righteous one, exercised this gift. We will consider discernment from the perspective of his own practice in the context of his monastic network. Here, we can glimpse how his fellow monks legitimated this gift through specific forms and acts of intercession. Explication of the marks of true discernment contained in the writings of Abba Ammonas permits us to imagine the reception of discernment and to explore the development of teachings about discernment in the context of the monastic network and so discloses how Abba Ammonas might have functioned as a physician of the soul for his brothers. Because his teachings on discernment are tied to the call for useful servanthood, we can consider how these teachings contributed to the construction of monastic activity, and of Christian discipleship, in this period.

Chapter 5 explores the expansion of these teachings to the members of the entire Christian community. Abba Ammonas and the members of his monastic network, like many others in his day, cultivated their monasticism in relationship with their local church, and so they were intimately aware and integrally involved in the workings of a larger Christian community. In this way, their practice of renunciation and virtue participated in the piety of the broader community. From this position Abba Ammonas, as one of many prominent spiritual fathers and as a specifically Egyptian one, envisioned how the monastic practice might help to facilitate religious renewal and reform in this period. A brief epilogue concludes this part of the book.

Part 2 provides English translations of Abba Ammonas' *Letters*, *Instructions*, and *Exhortations* as they have survived in Greek. Like the writings of many other monks of his day, Abba Ammonas' writings are found in a wide range of languages. The Syriac *Letters*, the earliest in date, have been accessible in English for over twenty-five years thanks to the work of Derwas Chitty and Sebastian Brock. The Greek *Letters*, *Instructions*, and *Exhortations* were printed in *Patrologia Orientalis* with a French translation by Francois Nau and have been unavailable in English.

This book is an introduction to the person and writings of Abba Ammonas and focuses on the model of spiritual formation he advanced in his historical, monastic, and ecclesiastical contexts. For this reason, it is not a prosopographical study, nor does it provide detailed analysis of his writings. As the state of scholarship on Abba Ammonas indicates, the need for such work remains. It is my hope that the narrow focus of this book will prompt others in the field to examine these writings for themselves and that future studies will assist the recovery and place-ment of this important early monastic thinker.

Notes

1. Ammonas, *AP* 11, in *The Sayings of the Desert Fathers: The Alphabetical Collection*, trans. Benedicta Ward, CS 59 (Kalamazoo: Cistercian Publications, 1975), 28.

2. Robert Kirschner, "The Vocation of Holiness in Late Antiquity," *Vigiliae Christianae* 38 (1984): 114.

3. Peter Brown, *The Making of Late Antiquity* (Cambridge: Harvard University Press, 1978), 94.

4. Richard Valantasis, *Spiritual Guides of the Third Century: A Semiotic Study of the Guide-Disciple Relationship in Christianity, Neoplatonism, Hermetism, and Gnosticism* (Minneapolis: Fortress Press, 1991), 3.

5. *The Lives of the Desert Fathers: The Historia Monachorum in Aegypto*, intro. Benedicta Ward, trans. Norman Russell, CS 34 (Kalamazoo: Cistercian Publications), 3. With regard to the act of reading the writings of the desert fathers, David Jasper writes: "we read not *through* the text, somehow consum-ing it in a search for its meaning, but read only by extending in ourselves the very existence of the text. In the oxymoronic text the saintly body becomes a

total presence only in its absolute self-forgetfulness, in pure kenosis, and thus the impossible imitation Christi, and impossibility which we therefore entertain in our reading" (*The Sacred Desert: Religion, Literature, Art, and Culture* [Blackwell Publishing, 2004], 29).

6. Philip Rousseau, *Ascetics, Authority, and the Church in the Age of Jerome and Cassian* (Oxford University Press, 1978), 24.

7. Rousseau, 25. In "The Ascetic Impulse in Early Christianity: Methodological Challenges and Opportunities," Vincent Wimbush suggests that "Christianity, certainly up to the fifth century in many circles . . . can with profit be understood and interpreted as counter-cultural, or at least counter-critical, as a complex of movements in opposition to the 'world.' 'World' in ancient Christianity was referenced with ambivalence: sometimes it referenced Satan in opposition to God's reign; at other times it referred positively to humanity and the natural, physical order . . . the resistance impulse obtained most consistently" (Elizabeth A. Livingston, ed., *Studia Patristica XXV: Papers Presented at the Eleventh International Conference on Patristic Studies Held in Oxford 1991* [Louvain: Peeters Publishing, 1993], 464).

8. Douglas Burton-Christie, *The Word in the Desert: Scripture and the Quest for Holiness in Early Christian Monasticism* (New York: Oxford University Press, 1993), 135. See also John Breck, *Scripture in Tradition: The Bible and Its Interpretation in the Orthodox Church* (Crestwood, NY: St. Vladimir's Press, 2001). Breck observes: "That is, the hermeneutic principles or rules of interpretation developed by the Fathers of the Church represent an extension and development of certain methods of interpretation that the apostles used to understand and proclaim the messianic significance of the Law and the Prophets" (34).

9. Ammonas, *AP* 8; Ward, 27.

10. Graham Gould, *The Desert Fathers on Monastic Community*, Oxford Early Christian Studies (New York: Oxford University Press, 1993), 26.

11. Gould, 27.

12. Valantasis, 3.

13. Rousseau, 20.

14. Ammonas, *Syr. Ep.*10; Derwas Chitty, ed. and trans., revised and introduced by Sebastian Brock, *The Letters of Ammonas: Successor of St. Antony* (Oxford: SLG Press, 1979), 13. The translation of the Syriac letters that is used in this study is Chitty's.

15. Laura Swan, *The Forgotten Desert Mothers* (New York: Paulist Press, 2001), 87.

16. Rousseau, 29.

17. William Harmless, *Desert Christians: An Introduction to the Literature of Early Monasticism* (Oxford: Oxford University Press, 2004), 172. See also Tomas Spidlik, *The Spirituality of the Christian East: A Systematic Handbook*, Antony P. Gythiel, trans., CS 79 (Kalamazoo, MI: Cistercian Publications, 1986), 284: "The great renown of the 'spiritual fathers,' the abbas, and the *startzy* (elders) in monasticism rests on the assumption that no one is any longer worthy to be enlightened directly by the Holy Spirit—although this would be in conformity with human nature—and especially, that not everyone is able to discern whether thoughts come from the Holy Spirit or not. . . . Spiritual direction is an obligation of the gnostic, 'the one who knows.' It is simply the discernment of spirits put into practice. Consequently, the gift of *diakrisis* (discernment) governs all others in the area of guidance. . . . The gift of discernment joined to that of 'prophecy,' being able to speak in the name of God, makes the perfect spiritual father." In addition, Laura Swan has aptly written that it was the task of the abba or amma to guide the disciple in the hope that he or she might obtain this gift too for "the amma journeyed and struggled alongside her disciple but maintained the detachment necessary for discernment" (Swan, 26).

18. Gould, 27.

19. Fulbert Cayre, *Spiritual Writers of the Early Church*, W. Webster Wilson, trans. (New York: Hawthorn, 1959), 82.

20. Kirschner, 112. In the same place he writes that by their "celibacy . . . identification with the poor . . . sufferings . . . confrontations with demons . . . night-long prayer vigils and miraculous healings" the monk conformed "to a highly specific model."

21. Hans J. W. Drijvers, "Hellenistic and Oriental Origins," in *The Byzantine Saint*, Sergei Hackel, ed. (San Bernardino, CA: The Borgo Press, 1983) 25–33, 25.

22. Spidlik, 284.

23. Edwin A. Judge, "The Earliest Use of *Monachos* for 'Monk' and the Origins of Monasticism," *Jahrbuch fur Antike und Christentum* 20 (1977): 72–89.

24. Bes, *HM* 4, and Theon, *HM* 6; Ward and Russell, 66, 68.

25. Augustine Roberts, *Centered on Christ: A Guide to Monastic Profession*, MW 5 (Kalamazoo, MI: Cistercian Publications, 2005), 35. See also Boniface Ramsey, *Beginning to Read the Fathers* (New York: Paulist Press, 1985), 164–81. With regard to the ideal of constant prayer among some of the desert fathers, Ramsey observes: "Sometimes this prayer could be practiced while working, but only if the work were of such a kind as to permit it. Thus it had to be simple, allowing the mind to soar of itself: consequently the weaving of baskets and the plaiting of mats, which required only mechanical movements, were much in favor. A monk could sit in his cell the whole day through, weaving baskets

out of reeds and reciting Psalms" (169). See also Robert Louis Wilken, *The Spirit of Early Christian Thought: Seeking the Face of God* (New Haven, CT: Yale University Press, 2003). Wilken draws specific attention to the significance of humility as a form of imitation in the thought of Gregory of Nyssa on pages 276–79.

26. See Timothy D. Barnes, *Athanasius and Constantius: Theology and Politics in the Constantinian Empire* (Cambridge, MA: Harvard University Press, 1993); see also David Brakke, *Athanasius and the Politics of Asceticism* (Oxford: Oxford University Press, 1995).

27. Barnes, 179. See also Peter Brown, *Society and the Holy in Late Antiquity* (University of California Press, 1982). Brown writes that the language of patronage draws on an established tradition of usage, and was employed in this period "because it was the idiom with which to conduct an obscure but urgent debate on the nature of power in Late Antique society and the relation of power to mercy and justice" (14).

28. Susanna Elm, *Virgins of God* (Clarendon Press, 1994), 254.

CHAPTER TWO

The Correspondence of Abba Ammonas

May God keep you in health of spirit and soul and body, till He brings you into the kingdom with your fathers who completed a good life, unto ages of ages, amen.[1]

A bba Ammonas' prayer honored the effort and legacy of those fathers who served as models for his audience. Through their affiliation with him, these monks had become members of a monastic network with an enduring heritage that defined their Christian identity. Correspondence, in the forms of personal visits and oral and written discourse, was critical to the development of this identity in its local context. This chapter presents evidence of forms of correspondence attributed to Abba Ammonas. While it may be inaccurate to speak in terms of an Ammonian corpus, and certainly there is no evidence that Abba Ammonas would have done so with regard to these sources, their preservation and transmission history allows us to treat them as representative of his thought. For this reason, their presentation will be followed by discussion of some of the methodological considerations inseparable from the use of these sources and which enhance our understanding of how they might have facilitated the maintenance and the advancement of the teaching and learning relationship between Abba Ammonas and his audiences. It was through these forms of correspondence that Abba Ammonas was able to teach a process of spiritual formation whereby the monk sought to attain the indwelling of the divine. In this way, his correspondence attests to the exterior paradigm that made possible such interior growth.

THE DESERT MONK

Little biographical information can be obtained about Abba Ammonas from his correspondence and from the traditional monastic sources of this period. Early affiliation with the Christian faith and possibly even monastic practice is indicated by a remark shared in one of his letters in which he called for a blessing from "the God whom I have served from my youth."[2] Longevity of monastic practice is suggested specifically by those sayings attributed to him in the *Apophthegmata Patrum*. There, Abba Ammonas is situated for at least fourteen years of his monastic practice in Scetis, a region below sea level with a harsh climate where ascetics were "guided by an experienced father or elder but living essentially as solitaries."[3] The *Apophthegmata Patrum* records an instance in which Abba Ammonas applauded this form of monastic practice before a visitor frustrated by his own restlessness. Upon finding Abba Ammonas the visitor asked: "'Three thoughts occupy me, should I wander in the deserts, or should I go to a foreign land where no one knows me, or should I shut myself up in a cell without opening the door to anyone, eating only every second day.' Abba Ammonas replied, 'It is not right for you to do any of these three things. Rather, sit in your cell and eat a little every day, keeping the world of the publican always in your heart, and you may be saved.'"[4] Further opportunity to affirm stability of practice and of place is found in his remarks to the audience of one of his letters, a group of monks whom he had recently visited. On this occasion Abba Ammonas supplied an uncommon glimpse into the chosen conditions of his own practice, conditions that concretized his advice. He writes: "And I want you to know that from the day when

I went forth from you, God prospered me in everything until I came to my place, and now that I am in my solitude He prospers my way the more and He helps me, be it secretly or openly. And I had wished that you should be near me for the sake of the revelations given to me. For every day these differ from the ones before."[5]

Although there is no indication he had any formal education, like other monks of his time Abba Ammonas was well versed in Scripture. His teachings derived from those found in the Hebrew Scriptures, the canonical gospels, and the Pauline epistles (including Hebrews and James) as well as in such apocryphal works as the *Apocalypse of Isaiah*.[6] The presence of this combination of works is not particularly significant given the state of the formation of Christian canon in the late fourth century.[7] We know that Abba Ammonas appealed to several sources by name in his letters, including repeated passages from the books of Psalms and Proverbs, but on occasion he admitted uncertainty as to the identity of a source as when he wrote: "Greet all those who are partakers in the toil and the sweat of their fathers in temptation, as John also says somewhere, 'By the sweat of the soul God is glorified.'"[8]

Evidence for Abba Ammonas' model of spiritual formation is found principally in his extant *Instructions*, *Exhortations*, and *Letters*. From the last of these "it is clear that Ammonas did not himself live in the community of monks for whom he acted as spiritual director."[9] His writings indicate that he was one of many monastic authorities with followers at varying stages of monastic practice in several distinct semi-anchoritic communities. Structurally, the monastic practice of his audiences would have been primarily a "solitary struggle under the guidance of a spiritual father and with the assistance of the prayers of the other solitaries of the same colony."[10] Among these, he appears to have guided some monks directly and to have offered insight to those whose practice was overseen by others. On one occasion, he admonished his audience "both in this and in other matters hearken to your teachers so that you make progress."[11] It is probable, then, that individual monks and groups of monks were the recipients of his counsel. Some of his letters are so closely related in tone and in theme that it is likely they affirmed the same issue for different audiences.

Letters of Abba Ammonas

Identification and publication of the extant writings attributed to many monks like Abba Ammonas occurred in the early twentieth century, a period that witnessed a burgeoning of scholarly interest in early Christian monastic practice. The recovery of Abba Ammonas' *Letters* in particular reflects the challenges these pioneering scholars faced and the opportunities their work provided for a deeper understanding about monastic practice. In 1914, Ludwig von Hertling undertook a study of the authenticity of the two Latin manuscript traditions of letters attributed to the fourth-century desert monk, Abba Antony of Egypt.[12] Von Hertling noted several internal inconsistencies in style and in content among these letters. The following year, Mihály Kmosko, working independently of von Hertling, found and edited the fourteen Syriac letters of Abba Ammonas.[13] Francois Nau edited the Greek text of these letters; his work appeared in 1915.[14] An important connection between the finds of these three scholars, namely that there were identical letters in the Latin and Syriac manuscript traditions, was made by Franz Klejna and published in 1938.[15]

Currently, there are French and English translations of the extant letters in Syriac. The French translation of the letters in this codex, edited by Bernard Outtier, has been published in a volume that includes the writings of several monks in this period, and the English translation was done by Derwas Chitty and revised with an introduction by Sebastian Brock.[16] Nau has argued that "it is certainly in Greek that Abba Ammonas spoke and wrote."[17]

Although it is not possible to offer a precise dating for the *Letters* of Abba Ammonas, an internal reference to Abba Antony and the explicit connection between the two monks indicated in the monastic sources suggests that they be dated to the middle decades of the fourth century. The transmission history of these letters confirmed what the traditional narrative sources had long taught about Abba Ammonas' relationship to Abba Antony. There are many references to a relationship between the two monks vividly depicted in the *Apophthegmata Patrum*. One saying records how Abba Ammonas, having lost his way while going to visit Abba Antony, was directed by divine providence.[18] Another depicts how

Abba Ammonas followed Abba Antony into the desert, watched him ask Moses to come and speak with him, and listened to their conversation, entirely unable to decipher its meaning.[19] Still another saying recounts that Abba Antony predicted Abba Ammonas' progress in the spiritual life thereby attesting further to some transmission of teaching between the two monks.[20] Direct evidence for this is found in one of the letters of Abba Ammonas in which he wrote: "Trials, therefore, are beneficial to the faithful, while those who have no experience of trials are untested; they wear the monastic dress but deny its meaning. For Abba Antony used to say to us: No man will be able to enter into the kingdom of God without trials."[21] Abba Ammonas made repeated appeal to the necessity of trials in his *Letters* and in his *Exhortations*. Whether or not the duplicate presence of this same teaching in a saying attributed to Abba Antony signals a borrowing, Abba Ammonas' attempt to situate it in this letter certainly suggests a shared interpretation of Scripture. Such localized meaning affirms what Douglas Burton-Christie has argued: that the use of Scripture among the desert monks addressed and responded to specific concerns. Burton-Christie writes that "the desert fathers stood within a well-established tradition of biblical interpretation . . . what was new and distinct about the desert hermeneutic was the peculiar combination of the locus of the desert and the questions that arose within the ascetical life there. The questions were shaped by the particular demands of the life; in turn, these questions affected the hermeneutic, both in terms of its substance and of its form."[22] As the most widely accepted monastic source of wisdom in the desert, Scripture and its interpretation was "always encountered as part of a lifelike situation."[23]

Abba Ammonas was one of many monks influenced by Abba Antony. The traditional narrative sources for the period attest to Abba Antony's association with other prominent monks. In his *Life of Paul*, Jerome drew attention to Macarius the Great (the Egyptian) and Amatas as the disciple responsible for the burial of Abba Antony.[24] Transference of spiritual authority between Abba Antony and some of the abbas of this monastic network is also found in the *History of the Monks*:

> In the Thebaid we saw a high mountain overhanging the river, a most awesome place with high crags, and we visited the monks who lived

therein the caves. Their father, whose name was Pityrion, had been one of Antony's disciples and was the second to succeed him as superior. He performed many different kinds of miracles and was especially noted for driving out demons. When he succeeded Antony and his disciple Ammonas, it was fitting that he should also have received the inheritance of their spiritual gifts.[25]

Inheritance and preservation mark the treatment of Abba Antony's teachings by members of this monastic network as well. Samuel Rubenson has argued that the abba's extant letters contain teaching retained and developed as specific to him after his death by his immediate followers and colleagues. This would make his letters "our main source for what can be termed the School of St. Antony, shaping lower Egyptian monastic theology."[26] False attribution of letters among the members of this network and the inclusion of teachings attributed to various members of this network in these letters attest to the common circulation and collection of their works and of their thought.

The *Letters* of Abba Ammonas, like many letters from this period, were written to impart or reinforce teaching and guidance. This expressly pedagogical purpose is shared by contemporary philosophical letters that sought to "affect the habits and dispositions of the reader" and "to instruct and direct the affairs" of their communities.[27] In many cases, the value of a letter was determined as much by function as by content. During the acute theological tensions of the fourth century, letters helped to maintain unity between individuals and among groups of monks. Letters were necessary for sustaining personal relationships between desert abbas and their audiences and were therefore useful for spiritual formation and guidance. Clearly, they are powerful evidence for the nature of Christian monastic community in this period: although apart, author and audience were still bound by clearly defined norms and practices and letters enforced and strengthened this identity.

The letters of monks like Abba Antony and Abba Ammonas emerged from the wisdom of their desert experience and acts of writing became opportunities to exercise that wisdom and to welcome their recipients into a relationship with the divine.[28] The evidence of monastic letters depicts how monks communicated with one another. The extensive use of Scripture in the *Letters* of Abba Ammonas and in those letters of his monastic colleagues show how Scripture served as the foundation for the language, diction, and content of monastic conversation. In their letters desert monks drew from the lives of Old Testament figures and lessons to underscore claims about the necessity of obedience and trust in God. Appeal to the early precedents of Abraham, Jacob, Moses, and Elijah also grounded claims of monastic authority. The gospel traditions and the Pauline epistles supported their exhortations to imitate the life of Jesus Christ. Scriptural support was offered, finally, in explanations of the purpose and reward of monastic life.

An attention to theological issues, Christian piety and ecclesiastical concerns often characterize Christian letters in the late antique period. The practice of letter writing in particular remained popular and necessary for the cultivation of ideas about these matters. Letters continued to retain their centrality of function in Egyptian Christianity, and letters served as a bridge between monks, clerics, and laity. Yet while written correspondence was a sufficient means of transmitting some types of information about monastic life, in certain instances the success of spiritual formation depended on an abba's willingness and ability to travel. Such occasions were often opportunities to solidify relations, to disseminate specific teaching or to offer guidance on those issues for which he believed written correspondence was an inadequate form of communication. After acknowledging the request for a visit to the correspondents of one letter Abba Ammonas wrote: "And so in your case, though you have been taught by the Spirit, yet if I come to you I shall strengthen you more fully by the teaching of that same Spirit, and shall make known to you other things which I cannot write to you in a letter."[29] Several times he went so far as to send one of his monastic colleagues to relay a message or to teach when he was unable to travel. Abba Ammonas' hope for assuring accurate interpretation is found in the conclusion of one letter in which he writes: "But this I have arranged, that my son should come to you, until our Lord grant to me also to come to you in the body, to give you growth greater than you have at present. For when fathers receive children, God is there on both sides."[30]

Abba Ammonas' own mobility figures prominently in several sayings in direct connection with his ability to serve as teacher. One saying records that while Abba Ammonas was on the river he spotted several monks on the banks who were looking for him. Immediately, he instructed the boatmen to bring him to shore where he greeted the monks and "having comforted their hearts, he sent them back whence they had come."[31] On another occasion, he used his decision to cross the river in the public ferry boat rather than in a private one to instruct that one "must walk in the way of God in peace."[32]

INSTRUCTIONS AND EXHORTATIONS OF ABBA AMMONAS

The *Instructions* of Abba Ammonas circulated in Greek, Georgian, and Latin. Their attribution is undisputed. The nineteen *Exhortations*, also extant in these languages, were transmitted with the *Instructions* in several of the Greek manuscripts. The Greek text of the *Instructions* and *Exhortations* was edited and published by Francois Nau in 1915.[33]

The extant *Instructions* of Abba Ammonas are organized around the single theme of repentance as a condition for prayer acceptable to the divine. The *Instructions* identify and briefly discuss the need for the cultivation of four virtues in conjunction with repentance. Each virtue is countered by its vice and contains appeal to the example of Jesus Christ. The first *Instruction* treats of humility, which is contrasted to pride.[34] Forgiveness of others is then followed by judgment.[35] The final *Instruction* reinforces that humility, forgiveness, and justice are vain exercises without charity.[36]

In a similar way, the *Exhortations* are evidence of efforts to systematize Abba Ammonas' teaching. Humility is the central theme that connects the *Exhortations*. Each exhortation is a reminder that humility is obtained by imitating Christ.[37] As Christ did, so the monk must do.[38] Several popular images of Jesus Christ and corresponding virtues are recalled to guide the monk's attempt: the humble demeanor of the slave, the silence of the sheep to be slaughtered, and the obedience of the servant. The *Exhortations* emphasize intention and action.[39]

The *Instructions* and *Exhortations* can be best categorized as paranaetic literature. In philosophical schools, paranaesis was "moral exhortation to follow a given course of action or to abstain from a contrary behavior."[40] Paranaesis "presupposed some positive relationship between the parties or that the one giving instruction was a moral superior."[41] Despite a multiplicity of forms in the ancient world "common techniques of paranaesis were reminding of what was known, complimenting what was done that was good, censuring wrong conduct, offering examples for imitation, stringing together brief precepts and admonitions, and giving reasons for the recommended conduct."[42] Many of these techniques appear in the *Instructions* and *Exhortations* of Abba Ammonas. It is likely that, as in other examples of paranaesis, the information contained in the *Instructions* and *Exhortations* pertains to the application of what is already known by the audience rather than to the presentation of new teaching. The *Instructions* and *Exhortations* addressed practical goals of education and moral formation. Their literary and thematic consistency likely enabled ease of recitation and memorization; such features may also have been the basis for adaptability, and this suggests how the *Instructions* and *Exhortations* may have functioned in meeting the needs of a specific community. The formulaic opening, continual emphasis on upholding the example of Christ, and the repetition of related images and phrases may have served as the kernel of each teaching; elaboration and expansion from this pattern to include material that met the needs or concerns of a local community could have been offered in the telling or repeating of the exhortation. In this way, the monks themselves were participating in the transmission of teachings that may have originated in the oral or written discourse of Abba Ammonas. We know, for example, that some of the Pauline letters were structured in such a way that practical or ethical instruction "followed the doctrinal exposition in the body of the letter and preceded the closing."[43] This form of presentation is found in philosophical letters as well. Certainly it is possible that some of the *Instructions* and *Exhortations* of Abba Ammonas circulated originally in the body of his *Letters*.

For Abba Ammonas and his audiences, the *Instructions* and *Exhortations* appear to have offered a succinct means of transmitting encouragement and clarification about core virtues of the monastic life. The counsel contained in these writings may have functioned as the framework for an early rule of guidance. Their practical emphasis and concerted focus speak to the lived experience of monastic practice, to the proper cultivation of those virtues required to know and do the will of the divine. In this, Abba Ammonas shared the contemporary efforts of many other spiritual fathers to craft guidelines for behavior oriented toward the social and spiritual dimensions of monastic practice. Sources akin to the *Instructions* and *Exhortations* would have provided a brief summary of some of the fundamental teachings that could be used for reference or for private recitation.[44]

Monastic Correspondence as Evidence

Abba Ammonas' writings were circulated and collected by those monks who had reason to do so. While their intentions may even have been connected to the depiction of spiritual formation these writings contain, we can only speculate about the vested interests that prompted their efforts. We do know that these writings, regardless of their intended addressees, were public documents. Often letters were addressed to the head of a community and were then read to all of its members. This practice was functional and practical. The use in the official church of the biblical texts, especially the wisdom literature, the Pauline epistles, and the gospels, is evident in debates over the determination of a Christian canon that peaked in the fourth century. We know, too, that desert monks also desired access to other texts even if that required the tedious task of translation from the original language of composition. Among the monks there was wide circulation of various genres and texts including homilies of the church fathers, the *Lives* of the saints, the apocrypha, the *Apophthegmata Patrum*, and the canonical literature.

The preservation of writings required the convergence of a number of factors. Many writings were lost because of the movement of monks and in some cases the destruction of monastic settlements. Thus it is difficult to speculate on the approximate total number of such writings on the basis of the few that remain. This, in turn, makes it nearly impossible to reconstruct with certainty lists of those writings that were in use within a given monastic network. While there were instances of cataloguing of writings, there is little indication that this was a standard practice in all monastic communities.

Given this set of circumstances, some things will remain unrecoverable in our study of the writings of Abba Ammonas. These writings contain his voice, perspective, and counsel. If we adopt the view of certain rhetorical theorists in antiquity for whom the letter was "a speech in the written medium" that would "reflect the personality of its writer"[45] then the writings of Abba Ammonas and his letters in particular are evidence of a conversation in progress. This is not to say that these writings took the place of conversation but, rather, that letters supplemented the words and visits of their authors. As Abba Ammonas reminded the correspondents of one letter, following a lengthy explanation of why they should exercise stability of place, "Do nothing therefore on your own, until I have come to *talk* with you."[46] Even when he delivered his message in the form of a letter it was often accompanied by personal contact through the sending of a messenger or the promise of a visit. In all of this, however, Abba Ammonas' audience remains silent. While we know that in some cases he wrote in response to their requests, we cannot recover their attitudes toward him, the perceived and realized value they assigned to his words, or their pattern of subsequent discourse and interaction with him in more than a hypothetical sense. On occasion, we can catch glimpses of these and this must suffice.

In spite of this, however, we would be sadly mistaken if we were to equate such silence with inactivity. Instead, such silence reflects further the nature of preservation and transmission. Certainly, Abba Ammonas' audiences were conversation partners. Hardly absent, passive recipients they were actively involved in steering the nature and form of his teaching. Abba Ammonas was prompted to write in response to their particular needs and thus the concerns he addressed reflect a specific local context. Even if it can only be recognized in a generalized sense, his concern for his audience and the living give-and-take of their relationship with him was a primary impulse for authorship.

Quite simply, the fragmentary and incomplete state of preservation does not reflect accurately the value of oral and written discourse in the desert. Both were stable means of communicating practical and spiritual concerns. The languages in which Abba Ammonas' writings were preserved and the complex transmission and translation history of these writings reflects an understanding of them as Christian documents with a private and public usefulness that was retained over time. To a certain extent this status increases the potential value of the information contained in these writings. It also complicates their use: to study these writings is to impose upon them a heuristic organizational claim that may hardly have been acknowledged by Abba Ammonas or by the monks of his day. Our study will therefore make appeal to many other sources. The narrative evidence for Christian monastic practice is wide and varied in genre, scope, and purpose. Furthermore, monastic ideas and practices emerged from contexts that they likewise informed. Yet, much of the literary evidence for Christian monastic practice in this period is marked by what Phillip Rousseau calls "propagandistic character."[47] That is, coupled with the didactic and eulogistic concerns in a given work is a propagandistic intent that may not have been the intent of the original authors as in the case of the *Apophthegmata Patrum* but of later editors.[48] Literature about ascetic behavior "was inspired by many different styles and models, and addressed itself to many different types of audience. It is a mistake to suppose that it originated and circulated only within a milieu that we could call specifically 'monastic.' Ascetic behaviour and reflection sprang from and operated within many different levels of Christian society. Even more important, the literature strives to defend or impose this or that attitude, this or that pattern of behaviour."[49] The historicity of the information in such traditional narrative sources as the *Apophthegmata Patrum*, the *History of the Monks*, the *Rules*, and the *Vitae* is suspect until and unless verified by nonliterary or other literary sources. As James Goehring writes, the "literature has rhetorical and ideological purpose."[50] Certainly, the same caution must apply to the *Letters, Instructions,* and *Exhortations* of Abba Ammonas although much is unverifiable. While these sources may differ in authorial intent and purpose their editors and compilers may likely have ensured that they, too, are not free of "rhetorical and ideological purpose."

Finally, despite the attempt of these sources to articulate through language the nature of religious experience of the mystery of the divine, they were always unable to express it completely. That is to say, their claims about experience were to some extent necessarily veiled, constrained, and inadequate. It is probable that such experiences were changed in the process of naming and expressing them. As Robert Louis Wilken has written of the pattern of Christian thinking in this period, early Christian theologians "wished not only to understand and express the dazzling view they had seen in Christ, by thinking and writing they sought to know God more intimately and love him more ardently. The intellectual task was a spiritual undertaking."[51] Desert ammas and abbas as well as those who wrote about them, drew heavily from a long tradition of like experiences recorded in Scripture in order to name and talk about their own experiences. For many desert monks their interpretation of the spoken or written word of Scripture enhanced and supported a personal experience of spiritual guidance and so their acts of compiling and transmitting the words of desert ammas and abbas became significant ways of preserving a depiction of spiritual guidance believed to be effective again through hearing and reading. In this way, the words and actions of these holy men and women were codified by many monks for the sake of defining and establishing individual and social identity thereby legitimating the monastic practice as a valid response to the Christian call to discipleship. Desert ammas and abbas, their deeds and their words, became symbols of spiritual realities accessible yet often unattainable by most Christians.

CONCLUSION

For Abba Ammonas and his audiences, the limitations language imposed in expressing the personal nature of spiritual formation and its effects was accommodated in part by an expansive understanding of the nature of monastic correspondence broadened to include written discourse as well as personal speech. The evidence of Abba Ammonas' correspondence allows us to consider the private and public dimensions of spiritual formation from the perspective of a leader in a prominent monastic network in this period. The monastic practice of the day entailed a lifelong process of purification, restoration, and adoption in which the desert abba, his disciple, and the divine operated coextensively and continuously. A clearly articulated concept of discernment lay at the core of this process. Our recovery and consideration of this process in the next chapter will then provide an opportunity to imagine how discernment was realized within his monastic network and the local Christian church community.

Notes

1. Ammonas, *Syr. Ep.* 3; Chitty, 5.
2. Ammonas, *Syr. Ep.* 7; Chitty, 9.
3. Armand Veilleux, "The Origins of Egyptian Monasticism," in William Skudlarek, ed., *The Continuing Quest for God: Monastic Spirituality in Tradition and Transition* (Collegeville, MN: Liturgical Press, 1982), 47.
4. Ammonas *AP* 4; Ward, 26.
5. Ammonas, *Syr. Ep.* 13; Chitty, 18.
6. See Joseph Blenkinsopp, *Opening the Sealed Book: Interpretations of the Book of Isaiah in Late Antiquity* (Grand Rapids, MI: William B. Eerdmans Publishing Company), 49–52.
7. See Hieromonk Alexander (Golitzin), "'Earthly Angels and Heavenly Men': The Old Testament Pseudepigrapha, Nicetas Stethatos, and the Tradition of 'Interiorized Apocalyptic' in Eastern Christian Ascetical and Mystical Literature," *Dumbarton Oaks Papers* 55 (2001):125–53. "Athanasius of Alexandria's festal letter of 367 did provide a list which corresponds to the Old Testament of the Hebrew canon, but the absence of the so-called deutero-canonical books and their persistence, for example, in the present day canon of the Greek and Roman Churches indicate that the canon was not fixed by the end of the fourth century. Further, at least two of the books to which Athanasius alludes in his epistle as apocryphal and even heretical, probably *1 Enoch* (and perhaps *2 Enoch* as well) and the *Ascension of Isaiah*, continued to be read in Egypt even as he was writing and, in fact, found their way into the very ample canon of Alexandria's daughter church in Ethiopia" (126).
8. Ammonas, *Syr. Ep.* 13; Chitty, 20.
9. Chitty, i.
10. Veilleux, 50.
11. Ammonas, *Syr. Ep.* 9; Chitty, 11.
12. Ludwig von Hertling, "Antonius der Einsiedler," in *Forshungen z. Geschichte d. innerkirchliche Leben* I, 56–60 (Innsbruck, 1929). See also Derwas

Chitty, *The Desert A City: An Introduction to the Study of Egyptian and Palestinian Monasticism under the Christian Empire,* third printing (Crestwood, NY: St. Vladimir's Seminary Press, 1999): "They are distinguished from the *Letters* of St. Antony, with which they were early apt to be bound up, by a considerable use of apocalyptic Apocrypha of which there is no trace in Antony, and by a development of the teaching about acquiring of the Holy Spirit which may have its analogies with Messalian teaching" (38). See also the comparison in Bernadette McNary-Zak, *Letters and Asceticism in Fourth-Century Egypt* (Lanham, MD: University Press of America, 2000), 17–47.

13. Michael Kmosko, "Ammonii eremitae epistulae," *Patrologia Orientalis* 10 (Paris, 1914), 567–616.

14. Francois Nau, "Ammonas, successeur de Saint Antoine," *Patrologia Orientalis* 11 (Paris, 1915), 432–64.

15. Franz Klejna, "Antonius und Ammonas: Eine Untersuchung uber Herkunft und Eingenart der Altesten Monchsbriefe," in *Zeitschrift fur katholischen Theologie* 62 (Innsbruck, 1938), 309-48.

16. B. Outtier with A. Louf, M. Van Parys, Cl.-A. Zirnheld, trans. *Lettres des Peres du Desert: Ammonas, Macaire, Arsene, Serapion de Thmuis* (Begrolles-en-Mauges: Abbaye de Bellefontaine, 1985); Derwas Chitty, ed. and trans., *The Letters of Ammonas, Successor to St. Antony,* revised with introduction by Sebastian Brock (Oxford: Fairacres Press, 1979).

17. Nau, 399–400. In support, Nau appealed to three cases of the use of Greek among those familiar with Abba Ammonas. He contends that it is probable that Pityrion, the second successor to Abba Antony composed his "numerous discourses" in Greek. Likewise, Moses the Ethiopian, a contemporary of Abba Ammonas, wrote in Greek to Poemen and to other monks. Finally, Nau asserted, it was in Greek that the *Life of Antony* was first composed.

18. Ammonas *AP* 7; Ward, 27.

19. Antony *AP* 16; Ward, 7.

20. Ammonas *AP* 8; Ward, 27.

21. Ammonas, *Ep. Syr.* 9; Chitty, *The Letters,* 11.

22. Burton-Christie, 61. See also John J. O'Keefe and R. R. Reno, *Sanctified Vision: An Introduction to Early Christian Interpretation of the Bible* (Baltimore, MD: Johns Hopkins University Press, 2005).

23. Burton-Christie, 61. See also Edward Shils, *Tradition* (Chicago, IL: University of Chicago Press, 1981). Shils' observation with regard to issues of transmission and interpretation of practices through time applies here as well: "The living forward into the present of beliefs and patterns of institutions which existed in an earlier time is a consensus between the dead and the living

in which the latter accept what the former have presented to them. The content of the consensus changes through interpretation; the consensus is maintained through the reinterpretation of what the earlier generations believed" (168).

24. Jerome, "The Life of Paulus the First Hermit," in *A Select Library of Nicene and Post-Nicene Fathers of the Christian Church. St. Jerome: Letters and Select Works. Series II*, vol. 6, trans. Philip Schaff and Henry Wace (Edinburgh: T & T Clark, 1893), 299.

25. Pityrion, *HM* 15; Ward and Russell, 99.

26. Samuel Rubenson, "Christian Asceticism and the Emergence of the Monastic Tradition," in *Asceticism*, ed. Vincent L. Wimbush and Richard Valantasis (New York: Oxford University Press, 1995), 53. Of the Arabic corpus, Samuel Rubenson has observed that the "attribution in this corpus of the letters of Ammonas to Antony is, although false, a sign of continuity in what could be termed a 'school of Antony.' A comparison of these letters with Antony's reveals how the theological tradition he represented was developed in the decades after his death" (Samuel Rubenson, *The Letters of St. Antony: Monastic Tradition and the Making of a Saint* [Minneapolis, MN: Fortress Press, 1995], 189).

27. Abraham J. Malherbe, *Moral Exhortation, A Greco-Roman Sourcebook* (Philadelphia, PA: Westminster, 1986), 79. See also Stanley Stowers, *Letter Writing in Greco-Roman Antiquity* (Philadelphia, PA: Westminster, 1986).

28. Often Abba Ammonas included reference to the claim in Proverbs 9:8 to "give occasion to the wise man and he will be yet wiser." On monastic letters, see Claudia Rapp, " 'For next to God, you are my salvation': reflections on the rise of the holy man in late antiquity," 63–82 in *The Cult of Saints in Late Antiquity and the Middle Ages: Essays on the Contribution of Peter Brown*, edited by James Howard-Johnston and Paul Antony Hayward (Oxford University Press, 1999). See also Irénée Hausherr, *Spiritual Direction in the Early Christian East*, CS 116 (Kalamazoo, MI: Cistercian Publications, 1990) where attention is given to the letters of several monks. There is little, if any, reason to imagine the Letters of Abba Ammonas functioning in a radically distinct way from the letters of his monastic colleagues. On those letters of Nilus of Ancyra addressed to laypeople, for example, Hausherr writes: "They often betray a concern with keeping them progressing in the ways of perfection; although, more frequently, they reply to questions about Scripture and theology" (312).

29. Ammonas, *Ep. Syr.* 5; Chitty, *The Letters*, 7.

30. Ammonas, *Ep. Syr.* 6; Chitty, *The Letters*, 8.

31. Ammonas *AP* 5; Ward, 26.

32. Ammonas *AP* 6; Ward, 27.

33. Nau, 455–71. The *Instructions* are found on pp. 455–58; the *Exhortations* are found on pp. 458–71.

34. See Ammonas, *Instructions* 1; Nau, 455.

35. See Ammonas, *Instructions* 2 and 3; Nau, 456.

36. See Ammonas, *Instructions* 4; Nau, 456.

37. See Ammonas, *Exhortations* 1; Nau, 458.

38. See Ammonas, *Exhortations* 1; Nau, 458.

39. See Ammonas, *Exhortations* 19; Nau, 471.

40. Everett Ferguson, *Backgrounds of Early Christianity*, 2nd ed. (Grand Rapids, MI: Eerdmans, 1993), 302.

41. Ferguson, 302.

42. Ferguson, 302.

43. Ferguson, 126. See also the discussion in Calvin Roetzel, *The Letters of St. Paul: Conversations in Context*, 2nd ed. (Atlanta, GA: John Knox and London: SCM, 1982).

44. The use of the *Instructions* and *Exhortations* in this way would entail a conscientious act of memory. See Mary Carruthers, *The Book of Memory: A Study of Memory in Medieval Culture* (New York: Cambridge University Press, 2008). Carruthers writes: "The choice to train one's memory or not, for the ancients and medievals, was not a choice dictated by convenience: it was a matter of ethics. A person without a memory, if such a thing could be, would be a person without moral character and, in a basic sense, without humanity. *Memoria* refers not to how something is communicated, but to what happens once one has received it, to the interactive process of familiarizing—or textualizing—which occurs between oneself and others' words in memory" (14).

45. Stowers, 61. See also Catherine Conybeare, *Paulinus Noster: Self and Symbols in the Letters of Paulinus of Nola* (Oxford University Press, 2000). Particularly apt in this context is her claim that "the self in late antiquity is, in a most thoroughgoing sense, relational" (17). With regard to patterns of silent reading exhibited by Saint Ambrose and witnessed by Saint Augustine, Alberto Manguel writes: "To Augustine, however, such reading manners seemed sufficiently strange for him to note them in his *Confessions*. The implication is that this method of reading, this silent perusing of the page, was in his time something out of the ordinary, and that normal reading was performed out loud. Even though instances of silent reading can be traced to earlier dates, not until the tenth century does this manner of reading become usual in the West" (*A History of Reading* [New York: Penguin Books, 1997], 43).

46. Ammonas, *Ep. Syr.* 11; Chitty, *The Letters*, 15. Emphasis mine.

47. Philip Rousseau, "Christian Asceticism and the Early Monks," in *Early Christianity: Origins and Evolution to AD 600*, ed. Ian Hazlett (Nashville, TN: Abingdon Press, 1991), 117. See also James E. Goehring, "Monastic Diversity and Ideological Boundaries in Fourth-Century Christian Egypt," *Journal for Early Christian Studies* 5, no. 1 (1997): 61–83. Here Goehring writes: "The ascetic tradition represented in the *Life of Antony*, the *Apophthegmata Patrum* and the Pachomian dossier has become, in a sense, a mythic history. It places the origins of Christian asceticism in an orthodox mythic past, made ever present through imitation, yet always beyond the imitator's grasp. The authors/compilers of the texts have fashioned acceptable literary icons. Conscious or otherwise, they created a powerful, self-perpetuating ideology. By rewriting ascetic history in terms of more rigidly defined doctrinal and ecclesiological boundaries, the famed ascetics of the past became sanctioned saints, and their imitation swelled the ranks of the ascetic movement as so defined" (78). This article is reprinted in his work, *Ascetics, Society and the Desert: Studies in Early Egyptian Monasticism* (Harrisburg, PA: Trinity Press International, 1999).

48. Rousseau, "Christian Asceticism," 116.

49. Rousseau, "Christian Asceticism," 116. See also Peter Brown, *Authority and the Sacred: Aspects of the Christianisation of the Roman World* (Cambridge University Press, 1997).

50. Goehring, "Monastic Diversity and Ideological Boundaries in Fourth-Century Christian Egypt," 61.

51. Robert Louis Wilken, *The Spirit of Early Christian Thought: Seeking the Face of God* (Yale University Press, 2003), 25–26.

CHAPTER THREE

The Monastic Journey

For he is careful to keep all his form living, that he may be counted in the inheritance of God.[1]

At the opening of most of his *Exhortations*, Abba Ammonas encapsulates a vision of spiritual formation wherein the soul progresses from its current state of separation from the divine toward complete union with the divine. The effort commences with, and is fueled by, a desire to become righteous, to achieve a state of perfection that requires submission to the Holy Spirit for education, trial, and testing. Successful passage leads to spiritual gifts. Worthy before the divine the monk may thereby be adopted as a son, gain entrance to the place of rest, and dwell there forever.

The purpose and structure of spiritual formation are among the many items addressed by Abba Ammonas. Given what we know about the forms of correspondence he employed and the fact that he addressed monks at varying stages of development, we may find it possible to reconstruct the elements of the journey of the soul from his *Letters* and to glean from his *Instructions* and *Exhortations* the rules of conduct that guided the monk. In each of these works, Abba Ammonas strongly encourages his audiences to follow him on the path to the Holy Spirit, a path of spiritual formation centered on purification, restoration, and adoption by the divine. Like those who had served him, Abba Ammonas sought to maintain continuance and development of this path through the activity of spiritual guidance. His requests for humility and obedience were intended to assure and assist those seeking to acquire the gift of discernment under the direction of the Holy Spirit.

MONASTIC EFFORT

According to Abba Ammonas, readiness for adoption requires first a purification of the body undertaken with the aim of effecting the unification of a divided self. He writes that "ever since the transgression came to pass the soul cannot know God unless it withdraws itself from men and from every distraction. For then the soul will see the adversary who fights against it."[2] Crippled by its inability to know the divine in its fallen, embodied state, the soul struggles in its blindness. Knowledge of the divine and the acquisition of new sight are possible for the soul because of the Incarnation.[3] Through obedience to the gospel paradigm of repentance and purification under the guidance of the Holy Spirit it is therefore possible for the desert monk to realize the fundamental Christian reality of salvation.[4] Perfect imitation through the monastic practice could redeem the soul's fallen state.[5]

Purification requires solitude or physical withdrawal to a place of geographical isolation. Unproductive in itself, solitude can foster awareness of the divine only when coupled with the cultivation of quiet. Solitude and quiet are willed by the divine as a means for healing and spiritual growth and are essential.[6] Abba Ammonas attributes his own progress to the cultivation of both and he warns that avoidance of solitude and quiet will prevent any form of spiritual progress, a claim based on the "many monks at the present time"[7] who "abandon quiet and remain in the company of their neighbors, receiving their comfort thereby, all their lives"[8] because they are overcome by "all the soul's sicknesses and distractions."[9] In contrast, quiet "heals on all sides"[10] as it enables a single-minded focus on God in every thought, act, and word.

The actual cultivation of quiet is multi-faceted. Several exhortations link quiet to acts of hearing, speech, sight, and touch thereby imbuing quiet with a tangible quality. It is important to note that Abba Ammonas does not teach the prohibition of such sensory acts but, rather, calls explicit attention to their proper purpose and use. When these purposes are recovered, such acts could empower the monk to live in a state of righteousness.[11] The monk's ability to *listen* well, then, depended on his hearing, speaking, seeing, and touching, too. Such acts may, in fact, acquire a distinctively reverent quality. For instance, in his exhortations about speech Abba Ammonas instructs not that his monks prevent speaking altogether but that they speak with knowledge of the sanctity of speech.[12] Abba Ammonas' instructions about when and how to speak ensure that the act of speaking becomes an exercise in humility before God and before one's audience. In this way, speaking can assume the quality of worship. The monk's dialogue with the divine, from the moment he feels the need to speak until the moment he actually does so, may become an act of sacrifice as the monk foregoes his own self-will in order to offer his motive for speaking, in humble deference, to the divine who then guides the utterance. Trained in its proper use, the monk was thus led to an understanding of the sanctity of speech.

Perhaps this is why Abba Ammonas also draws attention to those instances when silence is, in fact, preferred. If something distresses the monk or he has been wronged by another brother he should wait to use speech in response. Expressions of anger are to be avoided completely. The monk should address the situation first by prayer, and then he should pray for his brother.[13] If the monk feels the need to reprimand his brother but the brother is sorry and upset by his fault then the monk should say nothing.[14] In this way, any anger that the monk might know is thereby redirected and offered to the divine who then instills into the heart of the monk an appropriate response. Here, silence becomes a necessary component to speaking well.

Abba Ammonas' emphasis on the ability of prayer to dissolve or to silence anger may have derived from particular personal experience. A saying attributed to him, drawing further attention to the challenge posed by such action, records that he spent fourteen years praying for victory over anger.[15] Speaking well is possible only when the monk has listened well. That is to say, speech becomes a response to an act of hearing that itself requires training under the guidance of the divine. Although Abba Ammonas exhorted his monks against harmful speech,[16] they had to know how to address such content when it was heard. Again, in this situation, by offering what is heard to the divine, hearing might become an act of worship.

Abba Ammonas draws similar attention to the sanctity of sight. Since the vision of the eyes can disrupt the cultivation of quiet these too must be under supervision. Here as well, the monk must control both what he sees and how he sees it.[17] Once more, the sense of Abba Ammonas' words is didactic rather than punitive as his primary concern is that the monks preserve the sanctity of sight. It is not the eyes themselves but the concupiscence of the eyes that is of concern because in their proper state the natural function of the eyes is to see the divine everywhere. When the eyes are used properly, they function as they are intended for the glory of the divine. In this way, the monk's vision is a reflection of divine purpose.[18] The monk, as object of divine vision and as subject of human sight, is thereby offered a means of seeing well, as the act of seeing too may become an act of worship.

Abba Ammonas preserves the sanctity of touch in those exhortations that address manual works. The monk should remember that touch is reserved for those works of the body done in the service of God.[19] Manual works are those done in the service of the divine and in humility.[20] Through manual works the monk might thereby imitate divine humility in the example of Jesus Christ.[21] Working well so enabled the monk to maintain a pure body and precluded the demos from finding occasion to attack the monk.[22]

Abba Ammonas' rules of engagement pertaining to word, action, and thought are intended to create a proper spiritual orientation for the monk rooted in a hatred for things of the world and a heart free from impurities.[23] The cultivation of solitude and quiet enables a purification of the body to be done with knowledge of one's state of sinfulness and place of separation from the divine. Constant consideration of this urged the monk to remain steadfast in his efforts.[24]

Humility is the virtue, Abba Ammonas taught, closely connected to repentance. The exercise of humility guides the monk's choices and behaviors. Abba Ammonas admonishes the monk to act always as if in the presence of the divine.[25] Through the cultivation of humility, the monk may learn right relations not only before the divine but also in community with others. Abba Ammonas extends the practice of humility in this context when he exhorts that the monk is called to regard himself a servant of others.[26] Intended to educate and shape the worldview of the monk, the constant awareness of this relation to the world before the divine becomes the commencement of prayer.

Withdrawal, solitude, quiet, and acts of purification are all directed at the monk's effort to overcome self-will. Undue attachment to self-will, as well as the love of pride and pleasure, aggravates the soul's inability to see rightly. Through his efforts the monk attempts to create an undivided self as it performs works solely in accordance with the will of the divine. Such singleness of focus mirrors a singleness of purpose. In contrast, when the monk satisfies his self-will he acts of his own authority rather than under the will or authority of God. The result is a "dead body," and those monks who have such bodies are not accounted to be with God.[27]

The monk must continually struggle against the spirit of vainglory in an effort to make the body living and acceptable. This struggle is at the heart of desert monastic practice because vainglory is the primary obstacle for awareness of the divine will. Abba Ammonas taught that "as long as you do all that is in your power in making war on the spirit of vainglory, and strive against it continually, your body will be alive. For this evil spirit attacks man in every work of righteousness to which he sets his hand."[28] Close observation teaches that for those who are prideful, "the evil spirit immediately engages in battle with them, and overcomes some of them, scattering and quenching their body. In so doing it prompts them to leave their virtuous way of life, and involves themselves in pleasing men, thus destroying their body, though men reckon that they have gained something."[29]

Although the monk needs to be wary of drawing attention to his practice, this is often beyond his control. It is therefore the monk's response to such attention that is of concern, because such attention may develop into an opportunity for vainglory. The evil of such misdirected adulation is that it prevents the cultivation of humility and could draw the monk to fall ever further from the divine. Abba Ammonas emphasizes repeatedly that the monk redirect such attention to the divine in order that it might become another exercise in the cultivation of humility.[30]

Given the potential of vainglory to lead the monk astray, it is important that the monk learn to discern the source of his motivation and to
determine whether it was introduced by Satan, by the heart, or by the
divine. "Of these three, God accepts only his own."[31] Abba Ammonas
instructs that the monk may make this discernment on the basis of the
result of his action. If, for instance, the monk operates from a misguided
motivation his joy will be transparent and fleeting. Another measure
for differentiation can be observed directly because those who operate
under a false motivation, whom Abba Ammonas refers to as lax monks,
"have no fervor, but follow their own wills; and if they meet you, they
talk of the things of this world, and by such conversation they quench
your fervor. . . . For it is they who do not let people grow in spiritual
stature."[32]

It is clear from his teachings on solitude, quiet, and humility that
Abba Ammonas did not perceive the monastic practice as an isolated one.
That is to say, through his practice, the monk redefines his relations to
others and to his environment. Certainly, the highly sensory nature of
the monk's efforts discloses engagement with the created order. Indeed,
it is in and through interaction with the created order that the monk
attempts to listen well as the sensory acts of hearing, speaking, seeing,
tasting, and touching are regulated to the extent that their intention
becomes divine praise. The created order, and the place of the human
person in that order, is thus a vehicle for experiencing and knowing the
divine. As activities that enable participation in the created order, the
sensory acts articulated and described by Abba Ammonas are understood as gifts to be accepted and exercised in humility before the divine
creator. Abba Ammonas holds that the efficacy of such acts, and more
specifically the humility that they embody, extends beyond the individual monk. Trained to listen well to the divine, the monk's efforts bear
witness to the challenge of human frailty and to the hope of restoration.

DIVINE RESPONSE

Abba Ammonas advocates a monastic practice rooted in withdrawal
and renunciation; these allow for freedom from distractions and for the

cultivation of solitude, quiet, and acts of purification with the broader intention of listening well. If the monk denies himself and his own will through the cultivation of these and obeys his spiritual parents he becomes able to recognize the will of the divine. The monk should strive to acquire a divine power. This divine power is "the gift your fathers bore."[33] Abba Ammonas refers to it repeatedly as "the divine sweetness"[34] and as "the 'pearl' of which the Gospel tells us [cf. Matt 13:44], which was bought by the man who had sold all his possessions."[35] The divine power, a gift of the Holy Spirit, is given when the heart of the monk has become pure.

> If any man love the Lord with all his heart and with all his soul and with all his might, he will acquire awe, and awe will beget in him weeping, and weeping joy, and joy will beget strength, and in all this the soul will bear fruit. And when God sees its fruit so fair, He will accept it as a sweet savor, and in all things He will rejoice with that soul, with His angels, and will give it a guardian to keep it in all its ways as he prepares it for the place of life, and to prevent Satan from prevailing over it.[36]

To receive this protective divine power, the monk must first present himself to the Holy Spirit as a living body whose actions operate in accordance with the will of the divine and ask for it. Abba Ammonas guides the monks to "give yourselves to bodily toil and toil of heart, and stretch your thoughts up to heaven night and day, asking with all your heart for the Holy Spirit, and this will be given you, for such was Elijah the Tishbite and Elisha and all the other prophets."[37] This prayer must be offered from an undivided, upright heart, a "whole heart," that is, one that seeks the divine alone and is free from worldly cares and impurities. "But those who come to Him not with their whole heart, but in two minds, who perform their works so as to be glorified by men—such men will not be listened to by God in anything that they ask Him, but rather He is angry at their works. For it is written, "God has scattered the bones of the man-pleasers.""[38]

An upright heart is obtained in an act of purification by the spirit of penitence.[39] Once the monk has asked that the Holy Spirit come upon him, the spirit of penitence first overshadows the soul. After cleansing it, the spirit of penitence offers the soul to the Holy Spirit who, finding it pure, pours fragrance and sweetness upon it. This reward brings a certain joy to the monk, a fervor, which makes the monk despise all worldly attachments and gain sweetness in ascetic discipline. Upon receiving this joy, "everything that is done becomes thus sweet for them, until He has taught them everything."[40]

Yet, this fervor is also troubled, irrational, and temporary. Cleansed and educated by the Holy Spirit after the repentance and purification given in the gift of the first fervor, the monk is then handed over to Satan for testing. He writes:

> You must know how, in the beginning of the spiritual life, the Holy Spirit gives people joy when He sees their hearts becoming pure. But after the Spirit has given them joy and sweetness, He then departs and leaves them. This is a sign of His activity and happens with every soul that seeks and fears God: He departs and keeps at a distance until he knows whether they will go on seeking Him or not.[41]

Testing invites the monk to imitate the example of Christ, as Abba Ammonas instructs the recipients of one letter: "So when our Lord was incarnate and made in all things an example for us, when for our instruction in righteousness He was baptized and the Spirit came upon Him in the form of a dove, then the Spirit led Him up into the wilderness and delivered him to Satan to be tempted and Satan had no strength against Him."[42] The monk's imitation of this divine example is essential for spiritual growth. Abba Ammonas emphasizes this on several occasions as when he admonishes one audience to embrace trials, for "if trial does not come upon you, either openly or secretly, you cannot progress beyond your present measure."[43] Similarly, he instructs another audience that without trials "the soul cannot mount to the place of Life, that is, of Him who created it."[44] The monk should anticipate trials always.[45]

After giving the joy of the first fervor, the Holy Spirit departs from the soul and watches to see if the soul will continue to seek God. The divine "keeps at a distance until He knows whether they will go on seeking Him or not."[46] Trials give the appearance of abandonment and isolation to the monk. Without the presence of the Holy Spirit, "all the things which before had seemed sweet to him weigh heavy upon him."[47] In trials the body of a monk becomes laden with grief and boredom because it is burdened by the works of the divine. Some monks become so overwhelmed by their heaviness that they fail to ask that it be removed, and so they acquire a dead body "from love of vainglory and from pleasures."[48] For these monks temptation and trial are impossible to overcome and they fall into neglect by performing acts motivated from the self-will. Abba Ammonas cautions that such monks "wear the habit while denying its meaning. They are blinded in their eyes and do not recognize the work of God in them."[49]

For Abba Ammonas the choice posed to the monk either to surrender to temptation and in this to self-will or to remain steadfast and to seek obedience to the will of the divine has personal and social ramifications. The progress of the monk's own spiritual formation is at stake as Satan wrestles against him trying to deprive him of the blessing received. Yet, the state of humanity's progress toward the divine is also at stake for "it is impossible for Satan to try a faithful man unless God delivers him to be tried."[50] By divine providence, testing places the monk between the world as it is and the world as it is intended to be.

For successful passage, the monk need only realize that he is not alone in his trials. If in the midst of his trials he sees his fervor dissipating and perceives the heaviness in his body as something opposite to the joy he had known formerly he need simply seek it again and it will return. "And if you see your heart weighed down temporarily, bring your soul before you and question it until it becomes fervent again and is set on fire in God."[51] Abba Ammonas instructs one audience about how to do this by writing that the monk should "make a covenant between himself and God, and cry out in passion of heart and say to Him, 'Forgive me what I did in my neglectfulness; I will not continue in disobedience.' And then he should not walk any more as under his own authority in order to satisfy his own will, either in body or soul, but rather his thoughts should be spread out before God, while he afflicts and rebukes his own soul."[52] If his plea is made with tears and fasting from an upright heart and a denial of self-will, the monk shall secure passage from his trials. Such perseverance and prayer before trials is imaged in an account attributed to Abba Ammonas in the *Apophtheg-*

mata Patrum during which an unexpected encounter with a basilisk prompted supplication to God and immediate response: "by the power of God, the basilisk burst asunder."[53]

The monk gains successful passage through trials by his surrender of the self-will in absolute humility before the divine and in perfect imitation of the example offered by Jesus Christ in the wilderness. It is only by choosing to call for assistance from the Holy Spirit that the monk acts freely because this decision is in accordance with the divine will. "For when a man receives a blessing from God, at once his trial is increased by the enemy, who wants to deprive him of the blessing with which God has blessed him. For the demons, knowing that in being blessed the soul acquires progress, wrestle against it whether in secret or in the open."[54] On one occasion Abba Ammonas was compelled to share his own experience as evidence of this, an account of passage through his most recent trials in order to "make known in what temptation I have been, and what condition I now am in these days."[55] Knowing that he was tried by Satan but that this trial was sanctioned by the divine, his trial involved the descent of his soul into darkness which he described by comparing it to Christ's descent. As Christ descended, the atmosphere darkened and became heavier. Abba Ammonas writes that when he had been tempted in a similar way he glorified the divine "because He has lifted me up from that dark atmosphere and set me up upon the former height."[56]

The monk's conversion is embodied in his prayer for divine aid; his repentance, while built upon human effort, is a result of divine intervention. Conversion is the recognition of the truth that the monk struggles, not alone, but rather in solidarity with the divine. Abba Ammonas maintains that the monk's conversion brings a deeper indwelling of the Holy Spirit, a state of tranquility and single-mindedness. It is in this state that the monk is invited, and chooses, to participate more fully in the activity of the divine as conversion made perfect imitation of the example of Jesus Christ possible. Drawing on this example, Abba Ammonas reminds the audience of one letter, "You are they who have endured with me in my trials, and I establish with you the covenant of the kingdom, as my Father has promised me, that you should sit at my table [Luke 22:29]."[57]

DIVINE REWARD

As a result, the monk may receive a second fervor, a greater joy than the first, which is "peaceful, rational, and persevering."[58] This fervor "gives birth to the capacity in a man to see spiritual things as he struggles in the great contest, having a patience that is unperturbed."[59] The monk who receives this capacity "despises all dishonor, and all honor from men, hates all the needs of this world, hates all the comforts of the body, cleanses his heart of every foul thought and all the empty wisdom of this world, and makes supplication with fasting and tears night and day."[60] This divine power produces a joy that is with the soul continually and the monk will not toil in any matter. "Once you have received it you will pass all the time of your life in ease and freedom from care and you will find great boldness before God, which He will grant you."[61]

The monk who continues to cultivate the divine power and to have it dwell in his soul at all times, who maintains a heart free from defilement and vanities of this world and who conquers continually the spirit of vainglory by obedience to the divine in all things is transformed: "in these the Godhead dwells, feeding the soul."[62] Those who reach this state are rewarded for their labor with the riches of Christ, which are infinite. "And when you receive this Spirit, He will reveal to you the mysteries of heaven. For He will reveal many things which I cannot write on paper. But you will become free from every fear, and heavenly joy will overtake you; and so you will be as men already translated to the kingdom while you are still in the body, and you will no longer need to pray for yourselves but for others."[63] Such monks are made perfectly righteous and are "counted in the portion of the kingdom of heaven."[64] These souls are also awarded the Spirit of Truth, the "Comforter," and the Spirit that Christ gave to his servants, the apostles, that "dwells only in a few souls in each generation."[65] This Spirit was given "from Abel and Enoch unto this present day"[66] to those who are perfectly cleansed from all passions as "it is holy and cannot enter into an unclean soul."[67] To those in whom this Spirit dwells, "He will reveal great mysteries, and day and night will be alike for them. And He fills their spirit while they are yet in this tabernacle."[68] Having received the gift of discernment, that "great wealth of knowledge, which is the new vision," these souls are given the power to do what they were unable to do previously.[69]

With the cleansing of the soul by the spirit of penitence and the subsequent indwelling of the Holy Spirit in the first fervor, the soul gains a sense of divine goodness and sweetness. The final indwelling of the Holy Spirit, however, offers even more as it "wipes away and blots out the oldness of the 'old man,' and makes man to be a temple of God, as it is written, 'I will dwell in them and walk in them [2 Cor 6:17].'"[70] This final indwelling is a great aid in the return of the soul to God. "For just as trees do not grow unless the agency of water is available to them, so also the soul cannot mount upwards unless it receives heavenly joy."[71] Using imagery provided by the example of Jacob in the book of Genesis, he writes that after Jacob was blessed by his parents, "suddenly he saw the Ladder, and angels ascending and descending [see Gen 28]. And so now, as soon as men have been blessed by their fathers and have seen the hosts, nothing is able to move them."[72]

The Syriac corpus of Abba Ammonas' *Letters* includes a description of the ascent of the soul that has been identified with the apocryphal work, the *Ascension of Isaiah*.[73] "Thus, when the prophet was going to be taken up, going to the first heaven he wondered at its light; but when he came to the second he wondered so greatly as to say, 'I considered the light of the first to be as darkness;' and so on until the final stage of perfection. Therefore the soul of the perfectly righteous progresses and goes forward until it mounts to the heaven of heavens. If you have attained this, you have passed all trials."[74] The final indwelling is an indication of triumph, for when Satan, the evil one, "sees this guardian, that is, the power encompassing the soul, he flees, fearing to approach the man, and afraid of the power that is about him."[75] The final resting place of the soul is the place of life. As "children of the kingdom,"[76] the recipients of Abba Ammonas' writings could anticipate entrance into a final dwelling place. In one letter, there is the promise of dwelling in "the kingdom with your fathers who completed a good life."[77] In another letter, Abba Ammonas writes: "And I pray God for you, that He may keep you . . . until you depart from hence and He receives each one in a place where there is no grief nor evil thought nor sickness nor trouble, but joy and gladness and light forever, and paradise and the fruit that withers not and He receives you in to the dwelling places of the angels, and in to 'the Church of the first born who are written in heaven" [Heb 12:23].'"[78]

Hospitality Embodied

Abba Ammonas upholds that human sinfulness and divine redemption are the foundations of monastic practice. He advocates that physical withdrawal affords the soul the opportunity to ask unceasingly that the divine correct the soul and, in mercy, grant discernment. When the monk imitates the example of Jesus Christ by purifying the body, cultivating solitude and quiet, renouncing self-will, and immersing himself in constant prayer, then his soul might be worthy of an opportunity to see the evil encasing it and preventing it from union with the divine. An experience of grace, the reception of a divine power, and the indwelling of the Holy Spirit with which the soul gains the capacity to see spiritual things is part of the divine response to the human effort of the monk in these endeavors. To be counted in the inheritance of the divine is to have had one's sight restored, that is, corrected by a proper vision of a cosmos infused with the power and activity of the divine. The process of spiritual formation mirrors this activity to the extent that it is made possible by the divine who guides, directs, and rewards the monk; the monk is able to realize his complete dependence on the divine as the source and sustainer of all. Divinely sanctioned periods of testing are established not to discourage the monk but rather to reinforce an understanding of the providence, care, mercy, and love of the divine.

In Abba Ammonas' conception of spiritual formation the monk's effort to obtain a living body may suggest that Ammonas holds that there is an oppositional relation or division between the parts of the human person. This is not the case. For Ammonas there is a preexisting oneness among these parts that needs to be seen as such by the monk. Here, the human person is good and, while the monk may be called to engage in battle with the evil spirit of vainglory, this exists in a war between the divine and Satan that is played out on a cosmic level, not in the human person.[79] It is with this in mind that Abba Ammonas repeatedly likens the body to a tabernacle and to a temple. Such architectural metaphors symbolically represented sites of contact between human beings and the divine. In spiritual formation the effort to make oneself a holy site was motivated by a desire to create a place of hospitality. Through solitude, quiet, and ascetic discipline the monk attracts the attention of the divine who, through the monk's prayer, is invited to purify his body and soul. The monk who offers a body broken and desires restoration welcomed the divine as a guest.[80] As the divine leads the soul in a process of purification the monk works to make his body worthy of the divine indwelling through successful passage in trials and renunciation of the self-will. With the reception of the divine power the monk is guided by his divine host, the guardian of the soul, to the place of rest. Right relations between the monk and the divine are therein restored as the body of the monk is again a holy site housing the divine.

For Abba Ammonas, prayer is the language of hospitality; it initiates, sustains, and completes spiritual formation. And in this sense, spiritual formation is divine guidance bestowed in the act of prayer. According to Abba Ammonas, at the beginning of formation, the attainment of solitude, quiet, and humility introduces and engenders prayer as the continual dialogue of the monk with the divine. The monk prepares the soul by directing sensory acts properly. Distractions caused by misdirected attention render prayer ineffective. Prayer sustains the monk until he receives the indwelling of the Spirit and the final place of rest. While prayer assumes a multiplicity of form, when it is offered for reasons of praise, mercy, or spiritual gifts, prayer is at the encounter with the divine that is at the very center of spiritual formation.

The Spiritual Father

By bearing public witness to the activity of the divine in his own process of spiritual formation, the spiritual father holds a particular role in the education of the monk. "Despite Christ's injunction to 'call no man father' (Matt 23:9), early Christianity readily saw the human spiritual guide as sharing both the loving kindness of God the Father and the charismatic gift of the Spirit to engender others in the spiritual life."[81] Through prayer, the spiritual father invites the monk to renounce a worldview centered on the self-will for participation in one infused with the omnipresence of the divine. In prayer, the spiritual father is a model for how the monk may be righteous and live in a relationship of true discipleship before the divine. The spiritual father assists the monk in his effort to seek the divine and to imitate his ancestors in the faith by supplying instruction about the nature of the will, prayer, love, trials, and ascetic discipline. Through obedience to the wisdom and the word of the spiritual father such instruction guides toward an understanding of proper place before the divine. Collectively, Abba Ammonas' instructions about cultivating solitude, quiet, and obedience are primarily and essentially didactic; by incorporating the spiritual father's teachings about the relationship between divine will and self-will the monk learns how to have a living body.

Under the immediate direction of the divine, the monk is led to bear witness to the Holy Spirit as his direct spiritual guide. This unveiling of the operative power of the divine is then, over time, embodied by the monk in a transformation of status effected by the gift of promises to the monk who is now recognized as an adopted son or daughter and, as such, is handed over for the disclosure of divine mysteries. During all of this, the spiritual father prays that the monk receives the divine power and that he retains a living body; the spiritual father encourages the monk to maintain his righteousness so that he might then go on to be blessed in the place of rest. "I pray that the power of God may increase in you, and reveal to you great mysteries of the Godhead which it is not easy for me to utter with the tongue, because they are great and are not of this world."[82] Through relationship with a spiritual father the disciple might find a way to remain oriented toward the divine as his abba and guide.

Thus, as the body of the monk is transformed into a holy site, with the counsel of the spiritual father the monk learns to shift the focus of his prayer. Spiritual formation had commenced with the monk's own desire for the divine and his prayer that the divine enter his soul. Prayer is rooted in repentance, supplication, and humility.[83] In this way, prayer might thereby enable the monk to always give thanks.[84] Such internal focus directed at denouncing the self-will might thus create an upright heart and bring the monk under the direction of the divine.

We can now understand to some extent why Abba Ammonas used letters, exhortations, and personal visits to instruct and assist the monk fully about this process of spiritual formation. In his written correspondence Abba Ammonas was able to teach about the initial stage of this process as this could be articulated. Such correspondence functioned well, for instance, to explain how the monk might weigh a true motivation for action or consider whether a practice was rooted in humility. Correspondence also provided concrete advice and encouragement for specific stages of the monk's journey. Here, the *Instructions* and *Exhortations* were particularly beneficial. Their succinct form might have served the monk equally well in a time of confusion or joy because of the monk's relationship to their source and because of their constructive substance. The burden for their employment rested on the audience.[85]

The written word was limited, however, especially as the monk progressed to the later stage of the process of spiritual formation. Because this stage was under the direction of the Holy Spirit, Abba Ammonas could only describe the effects of such training. Thus, personal visits were required as these effects could not be articulated; they must be seen with eyes that had received new vision as Abba Ammonas instructed the recipients of one letter: "And I pray that I may come to you, that I may deliver to you also other mysteries, which I cannot write to you on paper."[86] While such visits afforded the opportunity to strengthen previous teaching about the living body, they did so with humble admission of its limits. "And so in your case, though you have been taught by the Spirit, yet if I come to you I shall strengthen you more fully by the teaching of that same Spirit, and shall make known to you other things which I cannot write to you in a letter."[87] Personal visits thereby verified and extended teaching in a highly particular way by validating publicly the reality of the experience of union with the divine for Abba Ammonas and his audiences. Though their own experiences of the divine were unique, their common recognition of its source and its effects affirmed the presence of this invisible, yet deeply present, reality.[88]

THE MONASTIC NETWORK

Abba Ammonas' conception of spiritual formation is consistent in many fundamental respects with what we know of the teachings of others in his monastic network. For example, obedience to the instruction of the Holy Spirit is a common feature in the letters of Abba Antony, who maintained that such instruction guided the monk to a gnosis, a knowledge that effected a harmonious ordering of relations between body, soul, and mind. This restoration of original relations within the self under the command of the Holy Spirit liberated the monk and led to further instruction and adoption.[89]

A similar conception of the work of the divine is also upheld in the *Life of Antony*.[90] The *Life of Antony* contains the core teachings of calling, repentance, purification, and restoration under the guidance of the Holy Spirit. In the *Life* the description of Abba Antony's acceptance of the call to the monastic life frames his link to a historical tradition; by releasing his possessions and withdrawing from society to the desert outskirts of his village, Abba Antony did as Christ had done before him by fulfilling the Gospel message to follow the will of the divine completely.[91] This link to historical tradition becomes grounded in existing constructions of monastic wisdom and authority when Abba Antony commences his practice by seeking the counsel of those established monastic authorities who had previously accepted a similar call. For Abba Antony, this entailed a journey to various locations just outside of his village near Alexandria in search of the holy men who lived there as hermits. After his visits, he would return to his own practice and, "recollecting in himself each person's ascetic practices, he zealously endeavored to manifest all of them in himself."[92]

Those who serve as Abba Antony's initial spiritual guides, the abbas of the *Life of Antony*, are depicted as facilitators who, once guidance is offered, are distanced from him. What is noteworthy is that this distance is followed not by the absence of a master to oversee Abba Antony's progress but rather by the replacement of a human abba with the divine as his guide. When Abba Antony's cultivation of the virtues he had learned prompts a series of trials from the devil, Abba Antony's faithful resolve and constant prayers provoke further testing. Shouting at Abba Antony, the devil finally confronts him directly: "I have deceived many, and I have brought down a multitude, but just now I was helpless in employing against you and your efforts the same tactics I have used against others."[93] Following a tirade of rebuke, Abba Antony responds:

"You are a despicable wretch, that is what you are, for you are black of mind, and you are a frustrated child. From now on I am not going to pay any attention to you, for 'the Lord is my helper, and I shall look upon my enemies.'"[94] The devil retreats, silenced by the abba's retort and profession of faith. As the narrative continues: "This was Antony's first contest against the Devil; or, rather, through Antony it was the triumph of the Savior."[95] Although the devil is overcome by the power of the divine working through Abba Antony, trials do not cease. His final assault from the devil takes place beyond the outskirts of the village in the tombs. At one point, the force of the devil's blows causes the abba to lay down and, from this position, to offer a prayer, beckoning the devil to torment him: "Look, here I am—Antony! I will not run from your blows! Even if you do worse things to me, nothing 'will separate me from the love of Christ.'"[96] As he is attacked and wounded, Abba Antony boldly challenges: "If you are able, and have received authority against me, do not hesitate, but attack now. But if you are not able, why do you bother me to no purpose? Our seal and wall of protection is our faith in the Lord."[97] This pronouncement prompts a specific type of knowledge of the divine.

> The Lord did not forget Antony's struggle at that time, but came to his help. Looking up, Antony saw the roof appear to open and a beam of light descend on him. Suddenly the demons vanished and the pain in his body immediately ceased and his dwelling was once again whole. Antony perceived the Lord's help, and when he took a deep breath and realized that he had been relieved of his suffering, he entreated the vision that had appeared to him: "Where are you? Why did you not appear at the beginning so you could stop my sufferings?" And a voice came to him: "Antony, I was here, but I waited to see your struggle. And now, since you persevered and were not defeated, I will be a helper to you always and I will make you famous everywhere." When Antony heard these things he stood and prayed, and he became so strong that he felt in his body more strength than he had had before.[98]

This statement of self-, and divine, disclosure marks a significant moment in the transformation of Abba Antony. The impact of his initial vocalization is heightened by the result. Abba Antony's statement discloses who he seeks to continue to be, namely, a being whose self-identity is revealed through the divine. Abba Antony, battling the devil in the isolation of his cell, appeals to the divine. When divine assistance is assured, the abba prays again, a public witness to a new awareness of the self as a being in intimate relationship with the divine. His prayer is evidence for the reader that he has become the embodiment of, and a mouthpiece for, the gospel message.

Dependence on the divine as abba and guide is heightened as Antony's knowledge is redefined by the personal experience of the human disciple before this divine master. It is in the midst of the human struggle to overcome trials, whether in the form of doubt or physical combat with demons, that knowledge of the divine, which consists of an intervention that affirms the ability of the monk to overcome the struggle, occurs. Because it rests on a recognition that the monk does not struggle alone but, rather, in solidarity with the divine, this knowledge also serves to validate and strengthen the monk. That is to say, knowledge of the divine effects transformation that brings to the monk a state of tranquility and single-mindedness and results in the reception of new gifts and abilities. The *Life* claims that, as a result, Abba Antony was in a state of utter equilibrium.

> After awhile, many people yearned for his way of life and wished seriously to follow his ascetic practice, while others, his friends, came and forcibly tore down his door and forced him to come out. Antony emerged as though from some shrine, having been initiated into divine mysteries and inspired by God. . . . When those people saw him, therefore, they were amazed to see that his body had maintained its natural condition. . . . The character of his soul was pure, for it had neither been contracted by suffering nor dissipated by pleasure, nor had it been afflicted by laughter or sorrow. Moreover, when Antony saw the crowd, he was not bothered, nor did he rejoice at so many people greeting him. Instead, like someone guided by reason, he maintained his equilibrium and natural balance.[99]

Like the *Letters* of Abba Ammonas, the *Life of Antony* upholds a depiction of the abba for the members of his monastic network. Both works contain a conception of the abba-disciple relationship whereby the human abba remains useful but not necessary to the journey of the struggling monk. Rather, it is human effort and the response of the divine that define the monastic practice as a form of Christian discipleship. Like the Antony of the *Life of Antony*, Abba Ammonas presents asceticism as a purification of body and soul in preparation for warfare overseen by the divine. In his *Letters*, Abba Ammonas had emphasized the role of the Holy Spirit as supervisor and as guide to the monk, a teaching retained in the *Life of Antony* where, as we have seen, those who served as Antony's initial spiritual guides were later distanced from him to be replaced by the divine. That is to say, the role of the human spiritual guide remained useful but insufficient to the journey of the struggling monk as, in both Ammonas' *Letters* and in the *Life of Antony*, transformation was restricted to the sphere of human disciple before divine master. Moreover, it was in the midst of the human struggle to overcome trials that transformation occurred and resulted in a state of tranquility and single-mindedness and in the reception of new gifts and abilities. Finally, the reception and role of a divine power, and the sense of abandonment by the Holy Spirit, are shared by Ammonas' *Letters* and the *Life of Antony*.

A Mysticism Defined

Common teachings might be situated in the context of a broader attempt to define the role of mysticism in the desert monastic practice of this period. The contents of the Syriac Codex of 534 CE, in which the *Letters* of Abba Ammonas are found, also includes works from Evagrius Ponticus, Pseudo–Macarius, and Nilus of Ancyra. While Abba Ammonas' thought was independent of the systematized program offered by Evagrius Ponticus and does differ from it in several important respects, including the goal of the mystical life as a supreme activity of the mind or intellect and the state of the soul's cleanliness before the indwelling of the Holy Spirit, both share the teaching that, once purified, the monk may be called to give service to others.[100] Furthermore, there is evidence in the Life of Evagrius of mystical ascent and the cultivation of discernment.[101] Additionally, despite the fact that key Messalian elements found in the writings of Pseudo-Macarius, such as the indwelling of the demons and the inefficacy of baptism, are absent from the writings of Abba Ammonas, both do describe the final indwelling of the Holy Spirit and union with the divine.[102] It is telling that the reception and role of a divine power, the Holy Spirit, and the journey of the soul's ascent are salient features in the teachings of Evagrius Ponticus and Pseudo-Macarius. Sometimes characterized in polar terms, these two strands of Christian spirituality coexisted and maintained for a period of time considerable influence on the development of a Christian mystical tradition.

Despite their distinctions, these teachers, like Abba Ammonas, emphasize the centrality of solitude and perseverance in prayer for the reception of the Holy Spirit, thereby stressing the inability of the soul to acquire this divine power on its own; the reception of this divine grace and the perfection of the soul can, though rarely, be reached in this lifetime. Furthermore, for each of these men, the debilitating effect of sin and the rehabilitating gift of the Incarnation are the foundation for the progression of the soul. Regardless of whether such analogies between the teachings of Abba Ammonas and those of Evagrius Ponticus and Pseudo-Macarius are best attributed to the common Syriac transmission and, hence, the possible influence of these letters, they may suggest foundational teachings in a broader mystical tradition within Christian monasticism.

Perhaps, then, we may understand the teachings of Abba Ammonas, whose central theme is "the acquisition of the Spirit, coming to perfect the purification and illumination of the monk's soul,"[103] as another independent strand in this tradition. As Johannes Quasten has observed that, apart from the *Apophthegmata Patrum*, the writings of Abba Ammonas "appear to be the most instructive and precious source for the history of the earliest monachism in the desert of Scete. The documents reveal an original and genuine mysticism, free of all system and theory."[104]

Conclusion

When Abba Ammonas encouraged his audiences to know the divine, he envisioned a way of being that cultivated solitude, quiet, prayer, and obedience to a spiritual father, and that required a pure soul and a request for the indwelling of the Holy Spirit from the whole heart. The earliest manifestation of this invitation had come during a moment of existential choice. When confronted with the divinely sanctioned abandonment of the Holy Spirit during trial and testing and the feelings of inadequacy, loss, and heaviness, the monk had to determine whether to remain as he was with a dead body ruled by the self-will and the passions and pleasures associated with pride and vainglory, or to renounce this way of being through faith and prayer for a living body obedient to and under the care, governance, and direction of the will of the divine. The monk's decision in that time of abandonment was pivotal because it was, for Abba Ammonas, essentially a decision for death in the world or life in the divine. The living out of its consequences defined Ammonian spirituality in terms of conversion, restoration, and adoption.

Like other members of his own monastic network, Abba Ammonas stressed the choice of Christian discipleship as it was embedded in the monk's experience of trials and testing. Spiritual formation entailed discipleship of Jesus Christ.[105] By withdrawal from society, purification, restoration, and adoption, the monk was called to discipline his body and soul and so to know the self in the presence of the divine. In this way, spiritual formation required a surrender of the self in order to reestablish natural, original relations with the divine.

In his own imitation of the example of Jesus Christ through the cultivation of a hospitable body, the spiritual father showed the monk how monastic discipleship was an expression of divine hospitality. In their relationship of guidance, the spiritual father and the monk were disciples of the example established by Jesus Christ. For Abba Ammonas, such commissioning in turn had invited the spiritual father and the monk to participate in the ministry of Jesus Christ and so in the salvific activity of the divine, thereby ensuring that, "The light of the righteous is never put out [Prov 13:9]."[106] It was through relationship with his audiences that Abba Ammonas extended his experience of divine love to them and so invited them to participate in the activity of the divine and to know Christian discipleship in its structural form and in its mystical end. In this way, Abba Ammonas describes two complementary dimensions of spiritual progress. He believed that his efforts as spiritual father facilitated the perpetuation of these dimensions by imitating the example of divine hospitality, thereby aiding "the sowing of God, and good sons are those who inherit our birthright and our blessing.'"[107]

Abba Ammonas attempted to do so in the context of the monastic relationship of spiritual guidance and the transmission of teaching about the monastic life. He appears to have offered a distinct emphasis on how the monk's experience of the divine, begun in his conversion as a transformation of identity effected during trial and abandonment by the Holy Spirit, was not for its own end but for the good of others as the spiritual father was sent again back into the world to serve as an agent of divine hospitality to the larger Christian community through the exercise of discernment. As we will explore in the next chapter, through this particular form of service, discernment was a gift shared; in the context of others, this gift became, as it was for Saint Paul, a public expression of divine hospitality intended to build and strengthen the corporate Christian community.

Notes

1. Ammonas, *Ep. Syr.* 1; Chitty, *The Letters*, 1.

2. Ammonas, *Ep. Syr.* 12; Chitty, *The Letters*, 16.

3. See Ammonas, *Exhortations* 1; Nau, 458.

4. See Ammonas, *Exhortations* 6; Nau, 463. See also Sr. Donald Corcoran, "Spiritual Guidance," in *Christian Spirituality: Origins to the 12th Century*, ed. Bernard McGinn and John Meyendorff (New York: Crossroad, 1985), 444–52. Corcoran's insight encapsulates this process: "All the effort of the desert elder was directed to increasing the receptivity of the disciple to the Holy Spirit" (450).

5. See Ammonas, *Exhortations* 1; Nau 458.

6. See Ammonas, *Ep. Syr.* 12; Chitty, *The Letters*, 17. Such a call hearkens to the observation made by Henry Chadwick, *The Early Church* (New York: Penguin Books, 1967), 178: "There was an ideological tension between the hermit-ideal and the belief that the monastic life required a community under

rule with obedience to a superior as an essential principle. In practice, there long continued to be numerous ascetics who were neither solitaries nor incorporated in a community (*coenobium*), but wandered from place to place, and were regarded as an irresponsible, disturbing element."

7. Ammonas, *Ep. Syr.* 12; Chitty, *The Letters*, 17.

8. Ammonas, *Ep. Syr.* 12; Chitty, *The Letters*, 17.

9. Ammonas, *Ep. Syr.* 12; Chitty, *The Letters*, 17.

10. Ammonas, *Ep. Syr.* 12; Chitty, *The Letters*, 17.

11. See Ammonas, *Exhortations* 7; Nau 464. In a more contemporary context, a similar sentiment on the spiritual life is expressed in Paul Evdokimov, *Ages of the Spiritual Life*, Michael Plekon and Alexis Vinogradov, trans. (Crestwood, NY: St. Vladimir's Seminary Press, 2002): "Essentially interior, it is also the life of man facing his God, participating in the life of God, the spirit of man listening for the Spirit of God" (57).

12. See Ammonas, *Exhortations* 18; Nau, 470.

13. See Ammonas, *Exhortations* 12; Nau, 466.

14. See Ammonas, *Exhortations* 12; Nau, 466.

15. Ammonas, *AP* 3; Ward, 26.

16. See Ammonas, *Exhortations* 19; Nau, 471.

17. See Ammonas, *Exhortations* 19; Nau, 471.

18. See Ammonas, *Exhortations* 12; Nau, 466.

19. See Ammonas, *Exhortations* 3; Nau, 460.

20. See Ammonas, *Exhortations* 11; Nau, 465.

21. See Ammonas, *Exhortations* 5; Nau, 462–63. Reference is to Mark 10:44. This conception of humility is reflected in Ammonas, *Instructions* 1.

22. See Ammonas, *Exhortations* 5; Nau, 462.

23. See Ammonas, *Exhortations* 2; Nau, 459.

24. See Ammonas, *Exhortations* 3; Nau, 460.

25. See Ammonas, *Exhortations* 10; Nau, 465.

26. See Ammonas, *Exhortations* 5; Nau, 462.

27. Ammonas, *Ep. Syr.* 1; Chitty, *The Letters*, 1. The idea that God does not accept the prayer of those who do their works from false intention is found as well in the *Instructions*.

28. Ammonas, *Ep. Syr.* 3; Chitty, *The Letters*, 4.

29. Ammonas, *Ep. Syr.* 3; Chitty, *The Letters*, 4.

30. See Ammonas, *Exhortations* 2; Nau, 459.

31. See Ammonas, *Ep. Syr.* 11; Chitty, *The Letters*, 15.

32. Ammonas, *Ep. Syr.* 4; Chitty, *The Letters*, 6.

33. Ammonas, *Ep. Syr.* 8; Chitty, *The Letters*, 9.

34. See for example, Ammonas, *Ep. Syr.* 2; Chitty, *The Letters*, 2; Ammonas, *Ep. Syr.* 3; Chitty, *The Letters*, 5; Ammonas, *Ep. Syr.* 12; Chitty, *The Letters*, 17.

35. Ammonas, *Ep. Syr.* 13; Chitty, *The Letters*, 18.

36. Ammonas, *Ep. Syr.* 2; Chitty, *The Letters*, 2.

37. Ammonas, *Ep. Syr.* 8; Chitty, *The Letters*, 9.

38. Ammonas, *Ep. Syr.* 3; Chitty, *The Letters*, 3.

39. See Ammonas, *Ep. Syr.* 13; Chitty, *The Letters*, 18.

40. Ammonas, *Ep. Syr.* 10; Chitty, *The Letters*, 13.

41. Ammonas, *Ep. Syr.* 9; Chitty, *The Letters*, 11. For close analysis of the development of Ammonas' teachings on trials in his letters, see David Brakke, "The Making of Monastic Demonology: Three Ascetic Teachers on Withdrawal and Resistance," *Church History* 70, no. 1 (March, 2001): 19–48: "In the *Letters* of Ammonas, we can see a monastic teacher developing his demonology in response to the changing conditions of his disciples and their relationship with him. Originally not a prominent aspect of his optimistic program of ascetic ascent to visionary insight, Satan and his demons become increasingly useful to Ammonas as his students encounter discouragement in their spiritual progress and exhibit disturbing desires for independence from their teachers" (40).

42. Ammonas, *Ep. Syr.* 13; Chitty, *The Letters*, 19.

43. Ammonas, *Ep. Syr.* 9; Chitty, *The Letters*, 10.

44. Ammonas, *Ep. Syr.* 10; Chitty, *The Letters*, 13.

45. See Ammonas, *Exhortations* 13; Nau, 467.

46. Ammonas, *Ep. Syr.* 9; Chitty, *The Letters*, 11.

47. Ammonas, *Ep. Syr.* 10; Chitty, *The Letters*, 13.

48. Ammonas, *Ep. Syr.* 1; Chitty, *The Letters*, 1.

49. Ammonas, *Ep. Syr.* 9; Chitty, *The Letters*, 11.

50. Ammonas, *Ep. Syr.* 13; Chitty, *The Letters*, 19.

51. Ammonas, *Ep. Syr.* 3; Chitty, *The Letters*, 5.

52. Ammonas, *Ep. Syr.* 10; Chitty, *The Letters*, 13.

53. Ammonas, *AP* 2; Ward, 26. The search of the early monks to know their place before and with the divine emerged from, and contributed to, a form of biblical interpretation as lived experience. As a result, early monastic literature is about encounter and relationship: those moments of contact with the divine and the means by which that contact is recognized, embodied, and embedded in human experience. Prayer and humility engendered the ability to listen well and to act rightly because they upheld the nature of the divine-human relationship.

54. Ammonas, *Ep. Syr.* 9; Chitty, *The Letters*, 10.

55. Ammonas, *Ep. Syr.* 13; Chitty, *The Letters*, 19.

56. Ammonas, *Ep. Syr.* 13; Chitty, *The Letters*, 19. On the expression of experience, see Luke Timothy Johnson, *Religious Experience in Earliest Christianity: A Missing Dimension in Earliest Christianity* (Minneapolis, MN: Fortress Press, 1998). Johnson writes that "experience is also invariably an interpreted reality, that is, the experience itself is at least partially constituted by the interpretation of the experiencing subject. Interpretation does not follow only after the fact, as though to clothe a naked encounter but is itself an essential component of the experience. It follows that language (in the broadest sense of that term) plays a role not only in the communication of experience to others but also and above all in shaping the experience as it occurs" (49).

57. Ammonas, *Ep. Syr.* 13; Chitty, *The Letters*, 20.

58. Ammonas, *Ep. Syr.* 10; Chitty, *The Letters*, 13.

59. Ammonas, *Ep. Syr.* 10; Chitty, *The Letters*, 13.

60. Ammonas, *Ep. Syr.* 2; Chitty, *The Letters*, 3.

61. Ammonas, *Ep. Syr.* 2; Chitty, *The Letters*, 3.

62. Ammonas, *Ep. Syr.* 6; Chitty, *The Letters*, 7.

63. Ammonas, *Ep. Syr.* 8; Chitty, *The Letters*, 10.

64. Ammonas, *Ep. Syr.* 7; Chitty, *The Letters*, 8.

65. Ammonas, *Ep. Syr.* 13; Chitty, *The Letters*, 18.

66. Ammonas, *Ep. Syr.* 13; Chitty, *The Letters*, 18.

67. Ammonas, *Ep. Syr.* 13; Chitty, *The Letters*, 18.

68. Ammonas, *Ep. Syr.* 13; Chitty, *The Letters*, 18.

69. Ammonas, *Ep. Syr.* 4; Chitty, *The Letters*, 6.

70. Ammonas, *Ep. Syr.* 10; Chitty, *The Letters*, 13.

71. Ammonas, *Ep. Syr.* 6; Chitty, *The Letters*, 7.

72. Ammonas, *Ep. Syr.* 6; Chitty, *The Letters*, 8.

73. Ammonas, *Ep. Syr.* 10; Chitty, *The Letters*, 12. This is identified in the note.

74. Ammonas, *Ep. Syr.* 10; Chitty, *The Letters*, 12.

75. Ammonas, *Ep. Syr.* 2; Chitty, *The Letters*, 2.

76. Ammonas, *Ep. Syr.* 4; Chitty, *The Letters*, 5.

77. Ammonas, *Ep. Syr.* 3; Chitty, *The Letters*, 5.

78. Ammonas, *Ep. Syr.* 1; Chitty, *The Letters*, 1.

79. See Nonna Verna Harrison, "Human Uniqueness and Human Unity," in *Abba: The Tradition of Orthodoxy in the West. Festschrift for Bishop Kallistos (Ware) of Diokleia*, ed. John Behr, Andrew Louth, and Dmitri Conomos, 207–20 (Crestwood, NY: St. Vladimir's Seminary Press, 2003). Akin to this view, Harrison writes: "Human nature must be understood not in negative but in positive terms, as a broader and more flexible concept than is sometimes supposed. Human nature is not a prison confining the person but a vast treasury of

resources available to the person's freedom, creativity and love, resources that can be used well or badly precisely by personal freedom but are in themselves good since they are created by God" (211).

80. See Ammonas, *Exhortations* 5; Nau, 462. In the ancient world, hospitality is specifically and uniquely centered in the guest-host relationship and it contains clear expectations and norms that are characteristic and distinctive. Hospitality "frequently begins with a welcome, then turns to restoration of the guest, followed by being with or dwelling with the other, and ends in the sending forth" (Amy G. Oden, ed., *And You Welcomed Me: A Sourcebook on Hospitality in Early Christianity* [Nashville: Abingdon Press, 2001], 145). Oden explains that "in the experience of hospitality both the host and the guest encounter something new, approaching the edge of the familiar and crossing it. Hospitality shifts the frame of reference from self to other in relationship" (25). With attention to the selection of students and disciples in the ancient world, see Ilsetraut Hadot, "The Spiritual Guide," in *Classical Mediterranean Spirituality: Egyptian, Greek, Roman, World Spirituality*, ed. A. H. Armstrong, 436–59 (New York: Crossroad, 1986). In the discussion of the selection of students by Seneca, Hadot writes that: "The individual effort—that is, the personal will of every person to develop the innate disposition to virtue—remains decisive. Where this will is absent and where the readiness to recognize one's own faults is lacking, every pastoral effort is condemned to failure from the outset" (450).

81. See Corcoran, 444–52, 447.

82. Ammonas, *Ep. Syr.* 6; Chitty, *The Letters*, 7.

83. See Ammonas, *Exhortations* 4; Nau, 461.

84. See Ammonas, *Exhortations* 16; Nau, 469. A contemporary parallel is found in André Louf, *The Way of Humility*, Lawrence S. Cunningham, trans., MW 11 (Kalamazoo, MI: Cistercian Publications, 2007). Referencing the temptation of Jesus in Matthew 26:41, Louf writes, "Two opposing forces confront each other here battling for control of the heart of Jesus and that of his disciples: the flesh, infirm and feeble, and the spirit that of a man but also that of God, both ardent, forceful and yet terribly encumbered by the pressures of the flesh. Jesus counsels two things: watchfulness and prayer. For it is at the heart of temptation more than anywhere else that the believer, already weakened by complicity with the flesh, experiences the necessity of God's aid: he cries out for help. It is there, at the center of the crisis (we are talking about a genuine crisis here) that a true humility, like a gift from the Spirit, is born. This humility alone allows the believer to pass through temptation with a minimum of risk" (24).

85. See Corcoran, 450: "The efficacy of the Holy Spirit depended on the mutual openness of master and disciple." With attention to the challenges of

spiritual guidance and spiritual fatherhood, John Chryssavgis reminds that: "Obedience and submission are qualities that may be *soul-purifying* for the disciple, but these very virtues of the disciple may become *soul-sullying* for the spiritual director. The elder must at all times be aware of limitations before God (whose divine will must be reflected), as well as of boundaries in relation to the disciple (whose free will must at all times be respected)" ("From Egypt to Palestine: Discerning a Thread of Spiritual Direction," in Behr, Louth, and Conomos, eds., 299–316, here 315).

86. Ammonas, *Ep. Syr.* 8; Chitty, *The Letters*, 9.

87. Ammonas, *Ep. Syr.* 5; Chitty, *The Letters*, 7.

88. It should be noted that such visits could be an opportunity for Abba Ammonas to serve as a confessor for the monks in his monastic network. As the monk proceeded in his spiritual formation, he would have required the service of a spiritual father with the particular ability to *listen well* and to discern faults in his attempts to keep a pure conscience. The inclusion of such a practice, implicit though it may be from the evidence of Abba Ammonas' exercise of discernment, certainly would have been consistent with the development of penance, the post-baptismal forgiveness of sin, in this period. By the fourth century, the duties of the confessor might be assumed by anyone deemed qualified by the Christian community, including a spiritual guide whose intercessory prayer was informal and pastoral in nature. Evidence for confession of faults is found in the Pachomian practice of the Remission, as well as among the *bnay qyama*, a Syriac-speaking Christian monastic group in the Persian Empire that has been described by Aphrahat in his *Demonstrations*. Such practices cultivated by the members of the *bnay qyama*, like that of the Remission in the Pachomian communities, attested to the mercy and forgiveness of the divine in monastic practice and afforded a means of maintaining that purity of heart essential to spiritual progress. Despite the distinctiveness of practice suggested by the evidence for each monastic community, it is certainly probable that the members of both would have employed some form of regular gathering as a corporate body in order to uphold public accountability for those faults and misgivings confessed in the private, daily purging of conscience of the individual monk before his spiritual guide. Given his emphasis on the role of purification, trials, and testing in the process of spiritual formation some form of these practices was incorporated into the life of Abba Ammonas' monastic network as well. As we have seen in our consideration of Abba Ammonas' exercise of discernment and the teachings about the limitations of human understanding and divine judgment this disclosed emphasize that this spiritual gift was intimately tied to individual and communal healing and reconciliation.

89. For the letters of Antony, see Derwas Chitty, revised and introduced by Sebastian Brock, *The Letters of St. Antony the Great* (Oxford: SLG Press, 1975). See also Samuel Rubenson, *The Letters of Antony* (Minneapolis: Fortress Press, 1995). Rubenson observes that Abba Antony's use of a variety of expressions for the Holy Spirit was "the result of a view according to which the activity of the Spirit in man is a process of growing participation, consummated in the granting of the 'fullness of the Spirit'" (80).

90. The translation and section marking that will be used here is Tim Vivian and Apostolos N. Athanassakis, *The Life of Antony*, CS 202 (Kalamazoo, MI: Cistercian Publications, 2003). Despite a complex redaction and transmission history, the *Life of Antony* preserves the depiction of Abba Antony as a teacher of gnosis and of the divine as the guide of monastic practice. See Samuel Rubenson, "Christian Asceticism and the Emergence of the Monastic Tradition," in *Asceticism*, ed. Vincent Wimbush and Richard Valantasis (Oxford University Press, 1995), 53. See also John J. O'Keefe and R. R. Reno, *Sanctified Vision: An Introduction to Early Christian Interpretation of the Bible* (Baltimore, MD: The Johns Hopkins University Press, 2005). The authors observe that "the hagiography of Antony exemplifies in narrative form Athanasius' vision of spiritual discipline and its role in the life of the church as a whole" (131).

91. In the earliest sections of the text, Antony has a conversion experience in the sense that he foregoes one way of being for another, a new identity in relation to self and others. This experience is carefully qualified in the work: it is the word (the gospel message) that leads to the experience and it is an experience that occurs in the context of the church. The stylized depiction of Antony as holy man is intentional and demonstrates "the extent to which the Lives which are recorded in the early Christian period are themselves model lives, portrayals of heroic individuals who are carefully presented to others for their imitation" (Averil Cameron, "On Defining the Holy Man," in *The Cult of Saints in Late Antiquity and the Middle Ages: Essays on the Contribution of Peter Brown*, ed. James Howard-Johnston and Paul Anthony Hayward, 27–44 [Oxford University Press, 1999], 37).

92. *The Life of Antony*, 4.2; Vivian and Athanassakis, 65. Antony's early practice models the historical reality of the earliest pioneers, those seeking to assume desert monastic practice would seek out the counsel of a practitioner. Discipleship was defined by the process of seeking out, and emulating, a desert monk. See also Augustine Roberts, *Centered on Christ: A Guide to Monastic Profession* (Kalamazoo, MI: Cistercian Publications, 2005). Roberts writes: "Among the first Desert Fathers and Mothers of Syria, Palestine and Egypt, there seems not to have been any explicit ceremony of initiation into

the monastic way of life. The life's characteristic features were embodied in the older monks for all to see. There was a permanent change of lifestyle, a clear separation from the structures and customs of the world of their time and the intention of continuing for the rest of their lives in this new state of following Christ in evangelical celibacy, simplicity, and prayer" (9).

93. *The Life of Antony*, 6.1; Vivian and Athanassakis, 71.

94. *The Life of Antony*, 6.4; Vivian and Athanassakis, 73.

95. *The Life of Antony*, 7.1; Vivian and Athanassakis, 73.

96. *The Life of Antony*, 9.1; Vivian and Athanassakis, 81.

97. *The Life of Antony*, 9.9; Vivian and Athanassakis, 83.

98. *The Life of Antony*, 10.1–11.4; Vivian and Athanassakis, 83–85.

99. *The Life of Antony*, 14.2–14.4; Vivian and Athanassakis, 92.

100. On the teachings of Evagrius Ponticus, see Andrew Louth, *Origins of the Christian Mystical Tradition: From Plato to Denys* (Oxford, 1981), especially 102–10. For a briefer treatment, see also James Harper, *Love Burning in the Soul: The Story of the Christian Mystics, from Saint Paul to Thomas Merton* (Boston, MA: New Seeds, 2005), 40–42.

101. See the *Life of Evagrius*, Tim Vivian trans., *Four Desert Fathers: Pambo, Evagrius, Macarius of Egypt and Macarius of Alexandria* (Crestwood, NY: St. Vladimir's Seminary Press, 2004), 86–88.

102. On the teachings of Pseudo-Macarius, see Columba Stewart, *"Working the Earth of the Heart": The Messalian Controversy in History, Texts, and Language to AD 431* (New York: Oxford University Press, 1991). See also Daniel Caner, *Wandering, Begging Monks: Spiritual Authority and the Promotion of Monasticism in Late Antiquity*, The Transformation of the Classical Heritage 33 (Berkeley and Los Angeles: University of California Press, 2002). With regard to Messalianism, John Meyendorff writes, "Messalianism was repeatedly condemned on several doctrinal counts, but particularly because it considered the knowledge of God a personal, ascetic achievement, independent of the sacred nature of the sacramental nature of the Church. The Church affirmed that, on the contrary, divine life and knowledge of God are gifts, both gratuitous and common to all the baptized, though also dependent upon personal spiritual effort" (John Meyendorff, *Rome, Constantinople, Moscow: Historical and Theological Studies* [Crestwood, NY: St. Vladimir's Seminary Press, 2003], 34).

103. *The Coptic Encyclopedia*, ed. Aziz S. Atiya, vol. 1 (New York: Macmillan, 1991), 113. Here, Lucien Regnault also writes that they are "among the few documents that tell us something about the mysticism of the desert fathers." While he appears to have shared much of the monastic theology and philosophical background of Abba Antony, Samuel Rubenson has observed that one of

the principal differences is the Ammonian concern with mystical experience. See Rubenson, "Christian Asceticism"; Rubenson, "*Ammonas-en Bortglomd Gestalt I Den Kristna Mystikens Tidiga Historia I*" in *Florilegium patristicum: en festschrift till Per Beskow* (Bokforlaget Asak, 1991), 168–85. Unfortunately, I was unable to consult this source.

104. Johannes Quasten further observed: "If we compare the correspondence of Ammonas with St. Antony's, the former is by far the more interesting" (*Patrology* 3, 191). André Louf later concurred by writing that, "L'interest principal des letters d'Ammonas est donc de nous presenter la premiere expression, rudimentaire encore mais d'autant plus precieuse, de la mystique des plus anciens Peres du desert" (See André Louf, "*Lettre attribute a Saint Ammonas*," Traduction francaise avec Introduction et Notes, in *Lettres des Peres du Desert: Ammonas, Macaire, Arsene, Serapion de Thmuis*, ed. B. Outtier, A. Louf, M. Van Parys, Cl.-A Zirnheld [Begrolles-en-Mauges, 1985], 9).

105. See Ammonas, *Exhortations* 1; Nau, 458. For further discussion in a variety of sources, see Corcoran, 444: "The Christian tradition has always emphasized that Christ or the Holy Spirit is the true guide of souls. We find here a notable difference from some of the other major spiritual traditions where the role of a spiritual master, teacher, or guide is central if not indispensable."

106. Ammonas, *Ep. Syr.* 7; Chitty, *The Letters*, 8. See Chryssavgis on the transmission and tradition of spiritual authority among abbas and disciples: "A deep awareness of the sacredness of this tradition maintained a strong sense of responsibility and accountability on the part of spiritual directors, primarily to God and toward their own elders from whom and through whom they received the gift of spiritual authority" (301).

107. Ammonas, *Ep. Syr.* 13; Chitty, *The Letters*, 20. See Irénée Hausherr, *Spiritual Direction in the Early Christian East*, CS 116 (Kalamazoo, MI: Cistercian Publications, 1990). Hausherr writes that "all spiritual direction consists in bringing another close to God through charity" (57).

CHAPTER FOUR

The Gift of Discernment

May the Lord keep you from this evil world, so that you may be healthy in body and spirit and soul. And may He "give you understanding in all things" [2 Tim 2:7] so that you may be delivered from the error of the time.[1]

Abba Ammonas' concern for the declining fervor and lack of discipline that he observed in the monastic practice of his audiences pervades his letters. On several occasions he shared his disappointment about the inability of too many monks of his generation to overcome their self-wills and to exercise right practice. To one audience he lamented that, "Not many monks or virgins have known this great and divine sweetness since they have not acquired the divine power, except some few have here and there. For they were not cultivating the power and therefore God did not give it to them."[2] Such laxity was evident in those "who come to Him not with their whole heart, but in two minds, who perform their works so as to be glorified by men—these will not be listened to by God in anything that they ask Him, but rather He is angry at their works."[3] At another time, Abba Ammonas advised against association with such monks and virgins claiming that "if they meet you they talk of the things of this world, and by such conversation they quench your fervor."[4]

Further teaching about one's neighbor was employed to counter the cultivation of improper interpersonal relations and the improper focus and direction they fostered. Abba Ammonas instructed the audience of one letter: "I know that the love of God is continually putting a man in mind of his neighbor. And our neighbor is he who is continually thinking on the perfect heavenly calling, praying for us night and day as for himself."⁵ In this context, the identity of one's neighbor appears to be based on a distinction between semi-anchoritic and coenobitic practice as elsewhere he refers to one's neighbor in terms that imply a distinctly monastic setting. Abba Ammonas mentions some monks who "live among men all the time, since they are unable to despise themselves and flee the company of men, or to engage in battle. Thus they abandon quiet, and remain in the company of their neighbors, receiving their comfort thereby, all their lives."⁶

The gift of discernment had provided Abba Ammonas with a new vision "to discern the difference between the good and bad in all things" and so to identify and address this state of monastic practice.⁷ Ammonas believed that, when cultivated, this gift fostered a particular way of perceiving the true purpose and function of human beings. When we examine those occasions in which Abba Ammonas cultivated discernment, like the audiences that received the words that open this chapter, we will see that it afforded him a means of instructing the members of his monastic community about the limits of human understanding and the nature of divine judgment.

DISCERNMENT DEFINED

This is particularly evident in one of Abba Ammonas' letters, which addresses a situation that appears pressing and requiring of immediate attention. Here, Abba Ammonas issued a stern warning about the consequences that would arise if a particular group of monks decided to leave their place of practice too soon because they felt called to return to the world. Knowing that they would be acting prematurely and from gross misunderstanding about the will of God for them, Abba Ammonas offered instruction about the nature of discernment and his own ability to serve as an interpreter of God's will for them. He opened the letter with a greeting that reminded the monks of his love for them and offered his motive for writing.

I hear that temptation is troubling you, and I am afraid it may come from yourselves. For I have heard that you want to leave your place; and I was grieved to hear it, though it is a long time since I have been seized by grief. For I know of a surety that if you go away from your place now, you will make no progress at all. For it is not the will of God; and if you go acting on your own authority, God will not work together with you nor go out with you, and I fear we shall fall into a multitude of evils.[8]

Indicators suggesting the level of Abba Ammonas' concern are found in both the tone and content of his opening. His fear and his grief are coupled with his certainty that their thinking is gravely flawed. Yet these serve as well to heighten his role as a site of discernment for them: his experience of these emotions is sudden and so contrary to his natural state; his certainty is unwavering and the basis for passing judgment on them.

In the remainder of the letter Abba Ammonas beckons his audience to recall the examples contained in Scripture about deception and the unrecognizable consequences of misunderstanding and then to examine their own motivations for action. Through his recollection of the decision of Eve, Abba Ammonas reminded them that deception can frequently arise from the pretext of better progress: "For when she heard, 'You shall be as gods' [Gen 3:5], by failing to discriminate the voice of the speaker, she disobeyed the commandment of God, and thus not only came by no good, but under the curse."[9] Likewise, he reminded them of Solomon's caution given to those who did not understand the will of God that, "There are many ways which appear good to men: but their end leads to the pit of hell [Prov 14:12]."[10] With the assistance of these models, Abba Ammonas then exhorted his audience to examine themselves and to establish whether their desire to leave was in accordance with the only acceptable motivation, one "sown by God in man."[11]

Abba Ammonas then explained that his own experience of the relationship between spiritual progress and obedience to his spiritual parents was further evidence of the veracity of his claims. Just as it was precisely because of his obedience that Jacob had received the blessing, Abba Ammonas reminded them, so too it was because of Ammonas' toil and obedience to his spiritual parents that God's will was revealed to him. In this way, their obedience to Abba Ammonas' appeal became an opportunity to practice renunciation and humility and to challenge their reluctance to remain steadfast in their obedience as he writes, "But I have heard that you have been saying, 'Our father does not know our labour, and how Jacob fled from Esau.'"[12] Abba Ammonas beckoned them to remember that Jacob did not leave his family of his own will but only when his father sent him away to Laban in Mesopotamia. In obedience and in spite of their desire to remain, Abba Ammonas advised, his audience should do the same: "Do not go away until God permits you. I am aware of what is God's will for you; but it is difficult for you to recognize the will of God. Unless a man denies himself and his own will, and obeys his spiritual parents, he will not be able to recognize God's will; and even if he does recognize it, he needs God's help in giving him strength to carry it out."[13]

Despite this guidance, however, Abba Ammonas appears to have remained concerned about their ability to recognize the will of God since he closed his letter by admonishing them again to stay in their place: "And if I endured great labour in the desert and the mountains, asking God day and night until God revealed His will to me, do you too now listen to your father in this, so that it may be for your rest and progress."[14]

Several stories about Abba Ammonas in the *Apophthegmata Patrum* illumine further how his exercise of discernment was a means of teaching his fellow monks about a right understanding of divine judgment. In one account Abba Ammonas refused to give a punishment to a young pregnant girl. Rather than judgment, the abba supplied the girl with a blessing by marking her womb with the sign of the cross. He also supplied her with six pairs of fine linens for fear that "when she comes to give birth, she may die, she or the child, and have nothing for the burial."[15] While her accusers continued to insist that Abba Ammonas mete out a penance to her, he silenced them by stating, "Look, brothers, she is near to death; what am I to do?"[16] Indeed, it is Abba Ammonas' course of actions rather than the situation of the girl that preoccupied the editors of the account and that guide its literary movement: transitions are marked by his tender treatment of her, his blessing of the child in her womb, his implicit reminders to the accusers that her judgment rests with God alone.

Another saying attributed to Abba Ammonas elicits a similar message. It recounts Abba Ammonas' encounter with a monk who was harboring a woman in his cell. When the monk heard that Abba Ammonas and several others were coming to see him, he hid the woman in a large cask.

> The crowd of monks came to the place. Now Abba Ammonas saw the position clearly but for the *sake of God* he kept the secret; he entered, seated himself on the cask and commanded the cell to be searched. Then when the monks had searched everywhere without finding the woman, Abba Ammonas said, "What is this? May God forgive you!" After praying, he made everyone go out, then taking the brother by the hand he said, "Brother, be on your guard." With these words, he withdrew.[17]

Here, Abba Ammonas' stern rebuke of those who judged the monk and his firm warning to the guilty monk upholds again, as in the previous saying, the belief that justice is the determination of the divine. Like the pregnant girl's accusers, the monks who investigated this cell responded to Abba Ammonas' words with silent obedience. Stripped of their power to judge because they have done so falsely, the accusers in these sayings were left to ponder their own distorted sense of relationship because it is, again, the distinctiveness of Abba Ammonas' course of actions that is upheld in the telling.

Abba Ammonas' teachings about the nature of judgment in these sources attest to the ways in which his exercise of discernment posed the challenge of living in right relationship with the divine and with one another as, in every case, his discernment of right relations was both didactic and pragmatic. By remaining steadfast in his practice the monk could continue to cultivate quiet directed to the will of God and so maintain a place in a community of fellowship and love. The monk's awareness of his inextricable relation to neighbor and to the divine ensured that his actions were governed by true charity.[18] Because it might prompt conversion to a new way of seeing one's place in relationship, Abba Ammonas' exercise of discernment could enable someone to realize the presence of the divine in the present setting to such an extent that they were moved from false judgment to an awareness of grace and love. Through word and action, Abba Ammonas imparted teaching that empowered his audiences to uphold the cultivation of humility and obedience for spiritual progress and the interpretation of discernment upon which these were based. The potential for transformation, however, rested not in the content of the teaching imparted but in the response of the audience to that teaching; that is, Abba Ammonas' exercise of discernment was efficacious only when it was accepted.

Abba Ammonas' understanding of the gift of discernment was contextualized by his own experience of it as a disciple. The members of his monastic network had defined themselves, in part, by their claims to a lineage of teaching about the nature and exercise of discernment, teaching that Ammonas would have been exposed to as a disciple and as a colleague of Abba Antony.[19] The letters of Ammonas' predecessor, Abba Antony, identify the spirit of discernment, a different phrase from that employed by Ammonas' successor, Abba Pityrion, as a specific spiritual gift.[20] The manifestation of Abba Pityrion's gift in teachings on the discernment of spirits probably reflects a development of thought within this monastic network. There is no evidence of the phrases discernment of spirits, or spirit of discernment, in the writings of Abba Ammonas. Rather, Abba Ammonas made use of the term "discernment" in a way that may have incorporated the sense of his predecessor and situated the later use of his successor.

For Abba Ammonas, discernment captured the highly specific sense of the abilities to discern between the self-will and the divine will[21] and to discern the difference between the good and the bad in all things.[22] In both cases Abba Ammonas' use of the term was qualified by reference to the same passage from Hebrews: "Solid food is for the perfect, who by reason of use have their senses exercised to discern both good and evil" (Heb 5:14).[23] Given this, it is probable that Abba Ammonas intended his audiences to interpret his use of the term in the context of this earlier use by Saint Paul where the ability to discern referred to the ability of those who are mature in the faith to appreciate and understand that which is true and to reject that which is false.[24] Just as Saint Paul exhorted his audiences to persist in their efforts to attain this state of understanding, in a similar manner Abba Ammonas admonished his audiences to persevere. Likewise, as Saint Paul served as a site of discernment for his audiences, having acquired a knowledge of the mysteries of the faith, so too did Abba Ammonas.

For Abba Ammonas this lineage of discernment was anchored in the examples found in Scripture of those righteous ones who had served as spokespersons for the divine in troubled times of deep separation. It is for this reason that Abba Ammonas brought the lives and the words of the prophets into the present context of the lived experience of his audiences. Parallels between their responsibilities and his certainly grounded his authority in the context of an established historical tradition. It was just as important, however, that such parallels defined the fallen state and promised redemption of his audiences as well. Abba Ammonas' audiences knew of the punishments that had been meted out to those who had chosen not to hear and to heed the warnings of the prophets; they knew, too, of the blessings rewarded to those who had listened well and repented. Through the voice and practice of the spiritual father, the divine issued an invitation to conversion; the decision to accept it rested in the heart of the individual person. So, like Isaiah, who informed the Israelites on behalf of the divine about the unacceptability of their fast, Abba Ammonas explained to those desiring living bodies the ramifications of actions performed for the sake of the self-will. Like Elijah the Tishbite, John the Baptist, and Elisha, Abba Ammonas instructed his audiences by words and through his practice about the withdrawal, bodily toil, and prayer necessary for the reception of the Holy Spirit.[25] As Ezekiel described the pattern of the perfect to those who sought new vision, Abba Ammonas shared the ascending journey of his own soul with those who struggled in their progress.[26] He also supplied examples of those who had experienced the gift of discernment. To one audience he wrote:

> And so now, as soon as men have been blessed by their fathers and have seen the hosts, nothing is able to move them. For when blessed Paul saw these hosts, he became unshakeable, and cried out and said, 'Who shall separate me from the love of Christ? Shall sword or famine or nakedness? But neither angels nor principalities nor powers nor height nor depth nor any other creature shall be able to separate me from the love of God [Rom 8:38].'[27]

Abba Ammonas frequently recalled the choices and the decisions of several members of this community of righteousness in order to illustrate both the lessons to be learned from their discernment and how the monk should respond. Illustration was always for the sake of instruction as Abba Ammonas invited his audiences to embody and to imitate the examples of these righteous ones. During trials, the monk should emulate the response of Abraham. Following Abraham's example, the monk "should not grow weary, but pray to God from your whole heart, giving thanks and showing patience in all things, and the trial will pass from you."[28] Likewise, the monk could imitate the example of David who, when he saw his heart weighed down by the withdrawal of the Holy Spirit prayed, "I have poured out my heart by myself [Ps 42:4], I have remembered the days of old, and meditated on all your works, I lifted up my hands to you; my soul thirsts after you as does a thirsty land [Ps 143:5-6]."[29] The monk who does this, Abba Ammonas instructed, will grow.[30] As we have seen in the letter to those who wanted to leave their place, the monk should consider carefully how Jacob's obedience to his parents was rewarded with the inheritance of the blessing of righteousness.[31] The permanent effect of Jacob's obedience, which enabled him to wrestle with the angel and prevail and to confront Esau whose heart was moved by the evil one against him without losing his blessing, should encourage the monk to seek the divine power.[32] Like Jacob, the righteousness of Joseph shielded him from later trials after his time in the prison, thereby attesting further to the benefit that awaited the monk's efforts.[33]

Clearly, Abba Ammonas believed that the gift of discernment had enabled him to enter into a community of righteous ones comprised of persons in every generation who were upright of heart and who had received the same Spirit.[34] This is captured in his words to one audience:

> Fathers according to the flesh leave to their children an inheritance of gold and silver. But the righteous leave this inheritance to their children: righteousness. The patriarchs were very rich in gold and silver, yet when they were near to dying they gave no other commandment to their children save about righteousness; for this remains to the ages of ages. Gold and silver are corruptible, and belong to this short-lived tabernacle; but righteousness is of that dwelling-place which abides to the ages of ages for man. Therefore the inheritance your fathers give you is righteousness.[35]

In and through prayer, Abba Ammonas extended an invitation to his audiences to participate in the life of this community as well. Such an invitation emerged from his belief that the gifts of the Spirit were corporate rather than individual in nature and, as such, they were for the purpose and benefit of building community. He acknowledged as much when he wrote of the righteous one that "as men already translated into the kingdom"[36] the righteous one no longer needed to pray for himself but for others. Through intercessory prayer, Abba Ammonas instructed one audience that he imitated the example given by Jesus Christ: "But I pray that you too may come to the place of life. And this I do because of your obedience. For when our Lord saw that His disciples obeyed Him, He asked His Father on their behalf saying, 'That where I am, there may they be also, because they have obeyed my word' [John 17:24]."[37] Thus, Abba Ammonas believed that Jesus Christ was present in a particular way in and through such prayer, prayer that emerged under the guidance of the Holy Spirit. He beckoned his audience to do the same:

> See, beloved, I have made known to you the power of quiet, and how it heals on all sides, and how God wills it. That is why I have written to you, that you may be strengthened in what you are doing, and know that it is in quiet that all the saints grew, and for this reason the divine power came to dwell in them, and made known to them heavenly mysteries; thus they drove away all the oldness of this world.[38]

Abba Ammonas appealed directly to the words of Jesus Christ in the gospel of John regarding this activity. "He used to say to them, 'If I depart, I will send to you the Comforter, the Spirit of Truth, and He will declare unto you all things' [John 16:7, 13]."[39] Likewise, in another letter, Abba Ammonas appeals to the example of Christ when he writes: "For when our Lord saw that His disciples obeyed Him, He asked His Father on their behalf saying, 'That where I am, there may they be also, because they have obeyed my word' [John 17:24]."[40]

Abba Ammonas' recollection of Saint Paul's love and prayer for those among his Christian correspondents in the churches in Asia Minor clarified further how he envisioned the role of prayer in the exercise of discernment. Saint Paul's unceasing prayer for the "great wealth of knowledge, which is the new vision, to be given to his sons whom he loved"[41] was the model Abba Ammonas offered to the correspondents of one letter: "Now, therefore, my beloved, since you have been counted to me as children, pray both day and night that this gift of discernment may come upon you, which has not yet come upon you since you came to this ascetic way. And I too, your father, will pray for you, that you may attain this stature."[42] Abba Ammonas followed a similar promise to the correspondents of another letter with the words, "For the blessed Paul also spoke thus in regard to those he loved, 'I am willing to give you not the Gospel only, but also our own souls, because you are so dear to us.'"[43] For Abba Ammonas, as for Saint Paul, these occasions were opportunities for celebrating life in the Spirit. After acknowledging the request for a visit to the correspondents of one letter, Abba Ammonas wrote: "And this is a very good thing. For Paul said, 'I desire to come to you, that I may impart to you some spiritual gift, so as to strengthen you' [Rom 1:11]. And so in your case, though you have been taught by the Spirit, yet if I come to you I shall strengthen you more fully by the teaching of that same Spirit."[44]

Saint Paul's relationship to Timothy provided a concrete model for the prayer by which Abba Ammonas reinforced his own relation to his correspondents as one of father to child rooted in a common faith community. Just as Saint Paul recalled the faith and tears of his disciple Timothy and desired to strengthen Timothy's faith by imparting spiritual gifts, so Abba Ammonas recalled the toils of the bodies and hearts of his beloved, promising to visit them in order to disclose mysteries that cannot be articulated. "For when Paul wrote to Timothy, who was counted among his children, he wrote thus, 'I remember you in my prayers night and day, greatly desiring to see you. For, recalling your tears, I am filled with joy; for I remember your unfeigned faith' [2 Tim 1:3-4]. And now, my beloved, as Paul did for Timothy, so I have done with you, calling to remembrance your sighs and heart's labors."[45]

As it did for his predecessors Moses and Saint Paul, the gift of discernment enabled Abba Ammonas not only to locate those with this vision but also to pray specifically for those who had not received it. Abba Ammonas prayed on behalf of those who were victim to old, or false, vision; through the exercise of discernment he identified the flawed understanding of an event or situation and suggested a means for rectification. Like Moses, he offered supplication. "For Moses, having received the Spirit, prayed for the people, saying to God, 'If you wipe them out, then wipe me out of your book of life' [Exod 32:31]. You see that his care was to pray for others having attained to such a measure."[46] On several occasions, Abba Ammonas also prayed on behalf of his audiences bearing witness that their hearts were upright.[47]

USEFUL SERVANTS

The evidence for the exercise of discernment by Abba Ammonas attests to how he, as a desert abba, imitated the example of Jesus Christ. As we have seen in our consideration of Abba Ammonas' exercise of discernment and the teachings about the limitations of human understanding and divine judgment, Abba Ammonas emphasized that this spiritual gift was intimately tied to individual and communal healing and reconciliation. Discernment was a means of establishing a living body, of ordering right relations, and of dwelling with others in accordance with the divine will. Through prayer, the products of discernment might sustain relationships of solidarity and Christian community before the divine.

Abba Ammonas believed that through imitation the monk might participate in a particular way in the activity of Jesus Christ in the life of the community: as Jesus Christ fulfilled the divine will so too the monk, in imitation of his example, might become a useful servant.[48] This recognition was an acknowledgement that the monk lived neither freely nor for himself but for the divine master.[49] For the monks of his monastic network, the exercise of useful servanthood, with humility as its base, yielded a love of God.[50] When it was lived under the guidance of, and in accordance with, charity, the monk might create solidarity with Christ through the exercise of humility.[51] Just as Christ humbled himself, so too the monk must exercise humility, the central virtue of useful servanthood.[52] Thus, the monastic call to useful servanthood required that Abba Ammonas' spiritual gift of discernment was manifest in a particular way. As a righteous one, Ammonas lived in imitation of the example set forth by Jesus Christ, and his relations with others mirrored the divine love Ammonas himself had received.

Ammonas' contribution was validated when others acknowledged his teachings and actions as a testimony to the constant activity of the Holy Spirit in the life of the Christian community.[53] The gift of discernment would remain alive in the life of the Christian community thanks to the lasting influence of useful servants like Abba Ammonas. Their example stressed that Christian discipleship was itself an imitation, empowered by the indwelling of the Holy Spirit of the Incarnate Word.[54]

Early Christians believed that the indwelling of the Holy Spirit greeted all those who underwent the transformation to new life promised in Christian baptism; it guided and directed them to a desire for deeper union with the divine. Through the celebration of the Eucharist, Christians were further united in a fundamentally Christian expression of love, peace, and hope. It is possible that it was through this fundamental union with all Christians that Abba Ammonas' monastic practice served the members of this local community and that such service as intercessor was distinctively ecclesiastical. That is to say, Abba Ammonas' monastic practice was a vocation in the Christian community because it contributed to and was in constant solidarity with the local community. "Hearing God's call, monks give up everything—property, possessions, family, friends—to live a life devoted to Christ. Their intention is to practice in love the fundamental virtues of the Christian faith (prayer, hospitality, charity, love, compassion, humility); they believe that all these gospel virtues are made flesh most completely by Christ."[55] In this way, the monastic vocation was distinct in form but similar in function to the vocation of any baptized Christian in this period to live the call of discipleship.

Patricia Cox Miller examines the ways Christian desert monks conceived the potential of desert space: "Enticing *and* forbidding, the desert was a place of both refuge and temptation, where the howling of wild beasts was heard along with prayers of the monks. Angels might dwell there, but so also did demonic forces. As a metaphor for the most basic makeup of the human, the desert exposed both angelic and demonic tendencies. The desert was thus a landscape charged with ambivalence."[56] If the desert was perceived as ambivalent space, then it was what was said and done there that transformed it. Indeed, as Peter Brown reminds us, the "anachoresis of the fourth-century hermit took place in a world that was exceptionally sensitive to its social meaning."[57] Crossing boundaries from their urban dwellings into wilderness space, pilgrims to desert monks participated in the exercise of discernment that marked and mapped such space, in the words of John Inge, as "the seat of relations and of meeting and activity between God and the world."[58] Writing on the sacramentality of place, David Brown maintains that, "Taking place seriously, therefore, must mean conceding that places too, like words, can have independent revelatory power despite all the ambiguities both share."[59] Just as with words, "so potentially then also with places. It is their capacity to develop a symbolic and imaginative reality that is larger than the construction of specific individuals that keeps their power alive."[60] Visitors to the desert monks contributed to the development and construction of desert space as a place of encounter with the divine. Regardless of the extent to which their arrival was motivated by expectation, curiosity, piety, or some other purpose, the presence and interactions of visitors and pilgrims were critical to the interpretation of desert space. With specific regard to pilgrims, "travelling to another place to see for themselves an alternative and better reality," the movement to and from desert space facilitated the creation of this space as a place of discernment.[61]

The overwhelming evidence for pilgrimage to holy women and men such as Abba Ammonas suggests how the monastic practice functioned as a visible, tangible model of Christian discipleship for individual Christians in this period.[62] Narratives of the period record stories marked by hospitality, wisdom, hope, and diversity of expression. Although there are accounts of some monastics, like Domnina, who would not return a glance,[63] there are accounts of others who would, and of the pilgrims and visitors who flocked to see them. Often a pilgrim would ask to pray with a monk or to touch the monk's garb. Pilgrims and visitors communicated with these holy men and women because they were perceived to be intermediaries and intercessors due to their reception of the gift of discernment.

These holy men and women were, for many, symbols of the holiness embodied in Christ; they exemplified what the Christian pilgrim was looking for.[64] Pilgrimage to a holy person could be imbued with a sense of the Christian past; enhanced by sense perception, the pilgrim claimed to encounter, through tangible means, a sense of the sacred. The exercise of discernment is frequently evident in the accounts of healing and of miracles that occurred on some of these visits. In his chronicle of the monk James of Nisibis, Theodoret writes, "So, too, he possessed prophetic foreknowledge of the future and received by the grace of the all-holy Spirit power to work miracles."[65] Other monks are characterized with the same gifts. Many pilgrims asked advice concerning future events and their willingness to see divine intervention through the virtue and holiness of the monk merited a reply. Faith healing, often exhibited through the laying of the hands of the monk upon the sick or the touch of a sacred symbol, produced similar results. Such experiences have a specific meaning in the context of the desert. "These events are not seen primarily as *mirabilia*, as things to be wondered at for their strangeness, as being contrary to the course of nature. They are signs, and signs of the power of God. They are, moreover, signs that God is working as strongly now as he did among the prophets and apostles. They illustrate the *virtus* of the monks, and place them directly in the line of the biblical revelation of the power of God."[66]

For many pilgrims, these monks had risen above human frailty and weakness and so represented the visible and tangible presence of the divine. Theodoret explains: "For the love of Christ constrains us, since we made this judgment, that one has died for all, so that the living might no longer live for themselves, but for him who for their sake died and rose again."[67] Desiring the love of the divine so completely, the monk felt called to recreate, through ascetic, human effort, the sufferings and sacrifice of Christ. Dying to self, as Christ had done, the monk made real the piety, virtue, humility, and obedience of a life physically and spiritually united in Christ; in this way, his perpetual union with the divine served as a viable path to holiness. In doing so, for many, the monk became a living symbol of what was possible through the Incarnation, and stood as proof for the presence and sustained activity of the divine. Writing about ascetics in the fourth century under Emperor Constantine, Philip Rousseau contends that, unlike many others, "they saw within their own society, with its disciplines, its abnegation, its withdrawal, its new sense of community and authority, the true fulfillment of the New Testament ideal, the true demonstration of what 'Church' should mean."[68]

For many, visits and communication with monks led hope-filled and inspired pilgrims to learn to incorporate intensely the wisdom of their experiences into daily life. Union with Christ through actions, words, and deeds was the route to Christian holiness, a necessary condition for salvation. To many early Christians, the attainment of salvation was dependent on a holy and exemplary life on this earth. The monastic practices made imitation possible. In this way these holy men and women performed a particular form of service seen in the relationships they fostered with the local Christian community. "Monasticism was a reminder that while the pledge and source of new life was the Eucharist and the grace it bestowed, still, acceptance of it was a free act of man, so that Christ's deed in no way diminishes human freedom or effort."[69] Symbolizing the eternal love of Christ in the world, the monk left his fellow Christians with a similar mission to embrace the call to love through holiness and devotion. Through purification, presentation to the Holy Spirit, and contemplation, the non-monastic Christian, like the monk, might become a living icon for the community and the society.

CONCLUSION

Examination of Abba Ammonas' model of spiritual formation has given us a fruitful way of exploring monastic practice as Christian action in this period. A reader of the letters and exhortations of Abba Ammonas encounters the way of a desert monk, a solitary one, who struggled earnestly to take refuge in a deep awareness of the divine as the source and sustenance of his being. While the seamless reality of Abba Ammonas' life is recoverable only in fragmentary pieces, his writings afford a sustained glimpse into an understanding of the role of the divine in the life of the monk that led him to formulate an accessible framework for a way of life that merged ascetic discipline and mystical union. As we have seen, for Abba Ammonas spiritual formation was a process whereby a monk underwent training in his quest for knowledge of and union with the divine. In his emphasis on the experience of the Holy Spirit, on the need to cultivate withdrawal, solitude, quiet, and prayer, and on the ascent of the soul, Abba Ammonas' model of spiritual formation illumines how discernment was acquired and how it might function in private and public expression as a means of helping others to respond rightly to the challenge of Christian discipleship.

Abba Ammonas' exercise of the spiritual gift of discernment in his teachings about human knowledge and divine judgment as found in his writings and in those sayings attributed to him and through his prayer enabled him to participate in this distinctive activity of the Holy Spirit. In turn, such discernment was evidence of a specific form of Christian monastic insight. As it did for other righteous ones who had come before, the exercise of discernment enabled Abba Ammonas to assist others in their attempt to see and define and know a true relation to the divine as abba and guide. As the embodiment of both process of acquisition and maintenance of its end, Abba Ammonas was a specific vehicle of instruction. His insight, and his ability to serve as a site of discernment, would have challenged others in his monastic network to live in a community of righteousness rooted in love. As a member of, and a contributor to, this community Abba Ammonas offered examples from his own experiences and from those of other righteous ones who had gone before him to the people of his generation. His witness was testimony to the lasting value of this community and to its efficacy in his own practice. In this way, Ammonas represented to others an alternative vision of the world and of their place in it, a glimpse at the divinely sanctioned order of creation, and welcomed the monk into communion with the divine. As we have seen, his ability to exercise discernment rested on the adoption of specific claims about prayer and tradition, claims that culminated in a vision of Christian discipleship as public witness to the mercy of God the Father, to the ministry of Jesus Christ, and to the spiritual gifts of the Holy Spirit.

NOTES

1. Ammonas, *Ep. Syr.* 1; Chitty, *The Letters*, 2.
2. Ammonas, *Ep. Syr.* 2; Chitty, *The Letters*, 2.

3. Ammonas, *Ep. Syr.* 3; Chitty, *The Letters*, 3.

4. Ammonas, *Ep. Syr.* 4; Chitty, *The Letters*, 6.

5. Ammonas, *Ep. Syr.* 5; Chitty, *The Letters*, 6.

6. Ammonas, *Ep. Syr.* 12; Chitty, *The Letters*, 17.

7. Ammonas, *Ep. Syr.* 4; Chitty, *The Letters*, 5. The early desert monks of Egypt wrote extensively about discernment as a gift of the Holy Spirit that was received as a mark of spiritual progress. Discernment made it possible for the monk to differentiate between good and evil in a specific context. Discernment was a gift to be shared; it was intended to assist others in their spiritual journeys. The early monks cultivated this gift by providing counsel and guidance to many persons of their day and, thus, served as sites of discernment for others.

8. Ammonas, *Ep. Syr.* 11; Chitty, *The Letters*, 14. For an exploration of monastic movement, see Maribel Dietz, *Wandering Monks, Virgins, and Pilgrims: Ascetic Travel in the Mediterranean World, A.D. 300–800* (University Park: Pennsylvania State University Press, 2005). Dietz writes: "Among the practices that arose during this period and in the absence of a commonly accepted paradigm of monastic behavior were a variety of forms of religious travel. Much of this early Christian travel focused not on a particular holy place, but rather on travel as a practical way of visiting living and dead holy people, and as a means of religious expression of homelessness and temporal exile" (2).

9. Ammonas, *Ep. Syr.* 11; Chitty, *The Letters*, 15.

10. Ammonas, *Ep. Syr.* 11; Chitty, *The Letters*, 15.

11. Ammonas, *Ep. Syr.* 11; Chitty, *The Letters*, 15.

12. Ammonas, *Ep. Syr.* 11; Chitty, *The Letters*, 16.

13. Ammonas, *Ep. Syr.* 11; Chitty, *The Letters*, 15.

14. Ammonas, *Ep. Syr.* 11; Chitty, *The Letters*, 16.

15. Ammonas, *AP* 8; Ward, 27.

16. Ammonas, *AP* 8; Ward, 27.

17. Ammonas, *AP* 8; Ward, 27.

18. See Ammonas, *Instructions* 4; Nau, 456.

19. Pityrion, *HM* 15; Ward and Russell, 99.

20. See Joseph Leinhard, "'Discernment of Spirits' in the Early Church," *Studia Patristica* 17, no. 2 (1982): 519–22; Bernadette McNary-Zak, "Transforming Monastic Authority in Fourth-Century Egypt," *Trivium* 32 (2000): 155–64. On the role of discernment in the *Life of Antony*, see Mark A. McIntosh, *Discernment and Truth: The Spirituality and Theology of Knowledge* (New York: Crossroad, Herder & Herder, 2004), 32: "Discernment is conceived of here as entirely a gift of the Spirit (though perhaps only granted to those prepared through 'much prayer and discipline' to receive it); and it is envisioned

as involving both the skill of identifying the variety of evil spirits, and the skill of knowing how each of them may be 'overthrown.'"

21. Ammonas, *Ep. Syr.* 11; Chitty, *The Letters*, 15.

22. Ammonas, *Ep. Syr.* 4; Chitty, *The Letters*, 5.

23. Ammonas, *Ep. Syr.* 4; Chitty, *The Letters*, 5. Ammonas, *Ep. Syr.* 11; Chitty, *The Letters*, 15.

24. See Victor Paul Furnish, *The Moral Teachings of Paul: Selected Issues* (Nashville: Abingdon Press, 1985). See also Nancy Caciola, *Discerning Spirits: Divine and Demonic Possession in the Middle Ages* (Ithaca, NY: Cornell University Press, 2003). Caciola explains: "For Paul, the discernment of spirits was a supernatural grace rather than a human endeavor" (5).

25. See Ammonas, *Ep. Syr.* 7; Chitty, *The Letters*, 8–9.

26. See Ammonas, *Ep. Syr.* 13; Chitty, *The Letters*, 19.

27. Ammonas, *Ep. Syr.* 7; Chitty, *The Letters*, 8.

28. Ammonas, *Ep. Syr.* 9; Chitty, *The Letters*, 11.

29. Ammonas, *Ep. Syr.* 3; Chitty, *The Letters*, 5.

30. Ammonas, *Ep. Syr.* 3; Chitty, *The Letters*, 5.

31. Ammonas, *Ep. Syr.* 7; Chitty, *The Letters*, 8.

32. Ammonas, *Ep. Syr.* 9; Chitty, *The Letters*, 10.

33. Ammonas, *Ep. Syr.* 13; Chitty, *The Letters*, 19.

34. Ammonas, *Ep. Syr.* 14; Chitty, *The Letters*, 21.

35. Ammonas, *Ep. Syr.* 14; Chitty, *The Letters*, 21.

36. Ammonas, *Ep. Syr.* 8; Chitty, *The Letters*, 10.

37. Ammonas, *Ep. Syr.* 7; Chitty, *The Letters*, 9.

38. Ammonas, *Ep. Syr.* 12; Chitty, *The Letters*, 17.

39. Ammonas, *Ep. Syr.* 13; Chitty, *The Letters*, 18.

40. Ammonas, *Ep. Syr.* 7; Chitty, *The Letters*, 9.

41. Ammonas, *Ep. Syr.* 4; Chitty, *The Letters*, 6.

42. Ammonas, *Ep. Syr.* 4; Chitty, *The Letters*, 6.

43. Ammonas, *Ep. Syr.* 6; Chitty, *The Letters*, 8.

44. Ammonas, *Ep. Syr.* 5; Chitty, *The Letters*, 7.

45. Ammonas, *Ep. Syr.* 5; Chitty, *The Letters*, 7.

46. Ammonas, *Ep. Syr.* 8; Chitty, *The Letters*, 10.

47. Ammonas, *Ep. Syr.* 8; Chitty, *The Letters*, 9.

48. See *Exhortations* 4; Nau, 461.

49. See *Exhortations* 13; Nau, 467.

50. See *Exhortations* 7; Nau, 463.

51. See *Exhortations* 1; Nau, 458.

52. See *Exhortations* 11; Nau, 465.

53. For an interpretation of the communal aspect of discernment in the letters of Saint Paul, see Luke Timothy Johnson, *Scripture and Discernment: Decision Making in the Church*, exp. and rev. ed. (Nashville: Abingdon Press, 1996), 109–32.

54. Again, the example of Jesus Christ, made possible by the Incarnation, was the Christian's model. The accounts in the canonical gospels record how Jesus Christ's baptism was followed by withdrawal to the wilderness for prayer. The temptations he encountered there were followed by his public ministry during which he traveled, preached, and performed miracles. He welcomed and loved the outcasts and unwanted of society.

55. Tim Vivian, trans., *Journeying into God: Seven Early Monastic Lives* (Minneapolis, MN: Augsburg Fortress Press, 1996), 7.

56. Patricia Cox Miller, "Jerome's Centaur: A Hyper-Icon of the Desert," *Journal of Early Christian Studies* 4, no. 2 (1996): 209–33, here, 210. See also Bernard McGinn, "Ocean and Desert as Symbols of Mystical Absorption in the Christian Tradition," *Journal of Religion* 74, no. 2 (April 1994): 155–81. McGinn writes that, "The monastic exodus out into the desert, however, could be taken both negatively and positively—as a journey into the abode of demons to do battle with the forces of evil or as a necessary separation in order to encounter God" (160). George H. Williams, *Wilderness and Paradise in Christian Thought: The Biblical Experience of the Desert in the History of Christianity and the Paradise Theme in the Theological Idea of the University* (New York: Harper, 1962), identifies: "(a) the wilderness as moral waste but potential paradise; (b) the wilderness as a place of testing or even punishment; (c) the wilderness as the experience or occasion of nuptial (covenantal) bliss; and (d) the wilderness as a place of refuge (protection) or contemplation (renewal)" (18).

57. Peter Brown, *The Making of Late Antiquity* (Cambridge, MA: Harvard University Press, 1987), 86. Brown continues, "It was a gesture that had originated in tensions between man and man, and the ascetic message derived its cogency from having resolved those tensions" (86).

58. John Inge, *A Christian Theology of Place* (Aldershot: Ashgate Publishing Company, 2003), 68. See also Henri Lefebvre, *The Production of Space*, trans. Donald Nicholson-Smith (Oxford: Blackwell, 1991): Some spaces are "devoted to encounter and gratification" (137).

59. David Brown, *God and Enchantment of Place: Reclaiming Human Experience* (New York: Oxford University Press, 2004), 161.

60. Brown, 162.

61. Brown, 162.

62. See Daniel Caner, *Wandering, Begging Monks: Spiritual Authority and the Promotion of Monasticism in Late Antiquity* (Berkeley and Los Angeles: University of California Press, 2002). Caner writes: "Christianization required that imaginations be reoriented toward new cultural icons, based not only on scriptural examples but also on living exemplars who vividly embodied the ideals that the Scriptures described. At the same time, church leaders had to acknowledge and accommodate the sensibilities of their large congregations, now being filled with the mainstream of Roman society. The pressures on these leaders to persuade and accommodate were exerted in turn upon a figure that rose to prominence in the rhetoric, literature, and society of the late fourth century: the Christian monk" (4). That this would continue into the sixth century is evident in Jennifer Hevelone-Harper, *Disciples of the Desert: Monks, Laity, and Spiritual Authority in Sixth-Century Gaza* (Baltimore, MD: Johns Hopkins University Press, 2005). Hevelone-Harper examines the letters of Barsanuphius and John: "The advice of Barsanuphius and John permeated the boundaries of the monastery and exercised influence in the private homes of lay Christians in the region. Lay people found the anchorites accessible, as demonstrated by the fact that more than a quarter of the letters in the Correspondence addressed the laity" (79).

63. Theodoret of Cyrrhus, *A History of the Monks of Syria*, translated with an introduction and notes by R. M. Price, CS 88 (Kalamazoo, MI: Cistercian Publications, 1985), 186–87. On the relation to pilgrimage as "a going away from all that held back the heart from following Christ" (4), see Benedicta Ward, *Pilgrimage of the Heart* (Fairacres Oxford: SLG Press, 2002). For the ways that this construction of space contributed to that of the desert body, see Patricia Cox Miller, "Desert Asceticism and 'The Body from Nowhere,'" *Journal of Early Christian Studies* 2, no. 2 (1994): 137–53.

64. See Isabel Colegate, *A Pelican in the Wilderness: Hermits, Solitaries, Recluses* (HarperCollins Publishers, 2002). Colegate writes: "It is difficult to be certain how the early Christian hermits felt about the actual desert in which they shared their daily lives, as opposed to the metaphysical one which they had chosen for spiritual reasons. Some seem to have feared it, others to have emphasized its harshness and desolation in order to magnify their own powers of endurance" (65). See also Mayeul de Dreuille, *Seeking the Absolute Love: The Founders of Christian Monasticism* (New York: Crossroad, 1999): "The Soldiers of Christ did not go to the desert to flee from the difficulties of the world but, on the contrary, to fight the enemy of the Church, the devil, on his own ground, in a personal struggle, as Christ had done" (37).

65. Theodoret of Cyrrhus; Price, 13.

66. Ward and Russell, 39.

67. Theodoret of Cyrrhus; Price, 195.

68. Rousseau, "Christian Asceticism," 118.

69. Alexander Schmemann, *The Historical Road of Eastern Orthodoxy*, trans. Lydia W. Kesich (Crestwood, NY: St. Vladimir's Seminary Press, 1977), 108.

CHAPTER FIVE

A Community of Discernment

Few are they who are made perfect. And these are they for whom are the great promises of the Son: they receive gifts and help men. For in every generation such men need to be found, who have attained to this measure that they may each of them be an example to the men of their generation as he who is counted perfect is an example to men.[1]

Abba Ammonas had instructed his monks that the monk confirmed in the final indwelling of the Holy Spirit could be called to leave his solitude and his quiet in order to bear, as a righteous one, a distinct form of witness to the mercy and love of the divine. Ammonas reminded the audience of one letter that, in the past as in the present, such men are called by the divine to serve in this capacity, as "all the saints who come among men to heal them follow the example of the Creator of all, so that they might be made worthy of adoption as sons of God."[2] The gift of discernment and the effects of the transformation produced in the heart and soul of the righteous one by the indwelling of the Holy Spirit were, in this way, to be extended for the benefit of others. On at least one occasion, Abba Ammonas provided clarification about the conditions under which such commissioning occurred. He wrote to the recipients of one letter:

They are only sent when all their own diseases are healed. For a soul cannot be sent into the midst of men for their edification if it has some

defect of its own. And those who go before they are made perfect go at
their own will and not at God's. And God says in reproof about such, "I
sent them not, but they ran of themselves" [Jer 23:21]. For this cause
they are neither able to guard themselves, nor to edify another soul.[3]

Thus, it was only after having been cured of infirmities and having
undergone training by the Holy Spirit that righteous ones could be sent
to serve others as "physicians of the soul" under the guardianship of,
and in accordance with, the mandate of the divine.[4]

The efficacy of such service depended entirely on whether it was in
accordance with the will of the divine. By disposing himself for others,
the righteous one bore witness "in grace and in joy and in love of men
and in love of the poor and good ways and in all the fruits of holiness"
and so participated directly in the activity of the divine.[5] In this way,
the righteous one received a particular opportunity to embrace anew
the world that he had formerly renounced and to serve as a testament
to the healing power and mercy of the divine in a fallen world.

The *Apophthegmata Patrum* contends that it was precisely the gift
of discernment that made Abba Ammonas particularly suited to service in a position of ecclesiastical leadership.[6] One story recounts
how Abba Ammonas trained under Abba Antony and continued on
his own to the point that he, Ammonas, experienced no wickedness.
It was because of this, the story continues, that he became a bishop
and was asked, as we have already seen, to pass judgment on a young
pregnant girl before her accusers. Authorized to issue a penance, he
exercised mercy, admonished her accusers, and sent the young girl
away with provisions for the birth of her child.[7] This account points
toward an important feature in the exercise of discernment in the life
of Abba Ammonas, in particular, and among many Christians in late
antiquity, in general. It suggests an expansive understanding for the
institutionalization of the cultivation of discernment as it is found in
the dual contexts of monastic leadership and episcopal office, in the
dual expressions of "physician of the soul" and "doctor of the church,"
and in the dual vocations of monk and bishop.[8] In order to consider
further how the spiritual gift of discernment may have functioned
in the broader context of the Christian community, this chapter ex-

plores the exercise of this gift by Abba Ammonas in his capacity as an episcopal authority.

An Episcopal Context for Discernment

We might begin to consider how discernment may have featured in Abba Ammonas' role as episcopal leader by returning briefly to some of the factors involved in the origin and development of ministry, and of ministerial offices, in late antiquity. Over a period of nearly three hundred years, Christianity had developed from groups of isolated communities located primarily in the eastern provinces in the first century to a cogent, highly recognizable, and tolerated religion traversing the entire Roman Empire and beyond, in the fourth and fifth centuries. In this process of transformation, believers assumed the tasks of sorting through considerable diversity in expression and practice in order to determine a standard rule of orthodoxy in canon, organization, and creed.

In the earliest Christian communities, the organizational model of the Jewish synagogue would continue to serve as the basic institutional foundation for the needs of its members.[9] Over time, governance by a body of elders, or presbyters, would be complemented by a range of other ministerial roles that emerged in order to address the specific needs of a given community. In the Corinthian community as it is described in 1 Corinthians 12:27-28,[10] for example, several leaders are identified:

> Now you are the body of Christ and individually members of it. And God has appointed in the church first apostles, second prophets, third teachers, then workers of miracles, then healers, helpers, administrators, speakers in various kinds of tongues. Are all apostles? Are all prophets? Are all teachers? Do all work miracles? Do all possess gifts of healing? Do all speak with tongues? Do all interpret? But earnestly desire the higher gifts.

A similar charge is also found in *The Didache*, or *The Teaching of the Twelve Apostles*: "Therefore appoint for yourselves bishops and deacons worthy of the Lord, men who are humble and not avaricious and true and approved, for they too carry out for you the ministry of the prophets and teachers. You must not, therefore, despise them, for they are your honored men, along with the prophets and teachers."[11]

Early evidence for the consolidation of many of these duties under the authority of a bishop can be found in a letter written by Ignatius of Antioch to the Trallians in which he describes briefly the visit to him of their bishop, Polybius, and the solidarity Ignatius felt with the entire Christian community through fellowship with him. Ignatius tells his audience:

> For when you are subject to the bishop as to Jesus Christ, it is evident to me that you are living not in accordance with human standards but in accordance with Jesus Christ, who died for us in order that by believing in his death you might escape death. It is essential, therefore, that you continue your current practice and do nothing without the bishop, but be subject also to the presbytery as to the apostles of Jesus Christ, our hope, in whom we shall be found, if we so live.[12]

There is considerable evidence for the sustained establishment of the episcopal office across the empire throughout the third and fourth centuries. The *Didascalia Apostolorum* illustrates the centrality of the bishop to the life of the Christian community by the third century.[13] The significance of the episcopal office articulated here is further exemplified in the experience of Cyprian of Carthage who responded to the deep discord of his audience during the Decian persecution. In his work, *On the Unity of the Church*, Cyprian explained that "the Church cannot, of its very nature be divided; for Christ signified that unity is of its very essence when he first entrusted to Peter alone that power of the keys which he later entrusted to all the apostles."[14]

After Emperor Decius died in 251 CE, and despite the persecution of Christians under Emperor Diocletian who issued a series of edicts against Christians in the early years of the fourth century, the Christian faith continued to grow. With regard to the Diocletianic persecutions, Noel King writes, "Terrible as it was to the Christians of the day, a latter-day wisdom can point out that [persecution] was never enforced Empire-wide, nor kept up consistently in any one place for a sufficient period of time, nor did it make effective use of the local and popular support which would have been easily available."[15] As Christianity grew, the church continued to gain the support of members of the upper classes. "By the end of the fourth century, the church, far from being a church of the lower classes, reflected the sharp divisions in Roman society: its upper echelons were occupied by highly cultivated persons, drawn from the class of urban notables."[16] Significantly, it had the support of political families like that of Emperor Constantius. The early Christian historian, Eusebius of Caesarea, takes care to record that with the political rise of Constantius' son, Constantine, "All men, then, were liberated from the oppression of the tyrant, and those who had been delivered from the miseries previously existing, acknowledged, one in one way, and another in another, that the only true God was the protector of the pious."[17]

With the legalization of Christianity under Emperor Constantine,

> clerical hierarchies were integrated into the political landscape: the bishop of the provincial capital (the "metropolitan") acquired authority over his provincial peers, while the bishops of the major imperial cities (Antioch, Rome, Alexandria, and Constantinople) became known as "patriarchs," first among equals, setting the stage for the later medieval developments of the papacy in the West and ecumenical patriarchate in the East.[18]

Those who convened at the Council of Nicea in 325 CE identified several pressing issues pertaining to the internal organization of authority in the Christian communities, as well as to the appointment and qualifications for those in the highest leadership roles. Due to conflicts within isolated Christian communities and with those outside of the church, several decisions regarding the hierarchical ordering of ecclesiastical administration were made. The conferring of the title, bishop, now had to be done in the presence of at least three other bishops.[19] Furthermore, there was to be only one bishop in each region.[20] In addition, regulations were created regarding transference to other sees.[21] Firmer structures, with penalties, were issued against any member of the clergy who sought, for example, to exchange offices, to flee his church, or to participate in lending money with interest.[22] Finally, as an early canon makes clear, there was a call for uniform understanding in liturgical duty and practice:

It has come to the knowledge of the holy and great council that in
certain places and in certain cities, deacons distribute communion
to priests, although it is contrary to the rule and custom to allow
the Body of Christ to be given to one who has the power to offer it
by someone who does not; it has equally been learned that certain
deacons take communion even before bishops. Therefore, let all this
come to an end, and let deacons stay within the limits of their assigned
roles, remembering that, on the one hand, they are the servers of the
bishops and, on the other, they are inferior to the priests.[23]

Coupled with this attention to uniformity of practice, there is evidence
of the formalization of the primarily liturgical role of the bishop and
the subordinate and accessory roles of the priests and deacons. Further
differentiation of roles is evident, as well, in the *Canons of Hippolytus*,
a collection of church rules from the fourth century, and in the *Testament of the Lord*. Both sources supply detail about the rituals and
practices surrounding other clerical offices such as the reader and the
subdeacon.

An emphasis on the liturgical function of the local bishop was further
accompanied by an increasingly prominent social role. David Batson
writes that under Constantine,

As the Christian community entrenched itself deeper in the fabric
of the empire, and the visible evidence of this was all around in mag-
nificent new buildings or sumptuously refurbished and converted
pagan temples, so the status of the bishops rose as leaders in society, as
protectors of the poor and as guardians of the rich, influential women
whose wealth could be directed into works of mercy.[24]

In this way, the duties of the bishop came to include responsibility
for hospitality to pilgrims, the care of widows, arbitration in disputes,
patronage, prayer, and protection of the poor.[25] Imperial support aided
the rise of the authority of the bishop and provided resources for the
expansion of the faith including attempts to disestablish pagan cult
and traditional Roman values. By the mid-fourth century, the Christian bishop was a highly visible member of the Christian community
and of Roman society. His office signified publicly those virtues that
differentiated and distinguished Christianity. Boniface Ramsey has

observed that in this capacity the bishop "represented in a visible way the unity of the local church."[26]

The definition of the episcopal office would include a role for the exercise of discernment, most prominent, perhaps, in the evidence of the bishop's involvement in issues related to health and healing. There is evidence that "during the third and fourth centuries, at least, the Egyptian Christian community generally had a highly developed interest in illness, health, and healing, perhaps more so than in any other Christian communities for which we have historical data. Papyrological evidence, while it cannot be used for comparative purposes, also testifies to the very significant interest in this theme among Egyptian Christians."[27]

For the purpose of more fully understanding how Abba Ammonas might have incorporated the gift of discernment as a bishop, we might consider the impact of the political position of the monk-bishop on the cultivation of a discernment of healing in the Christian community. In their study of caring and curing in the early Christian tradition, Darrel Amundsen and Gary Ferngren observe that while "concern for the ill was urged upon all Christians in the early church, it increasingly became the specific duty of deacons and deaconesses to report cases of sickness or poverty to the local bishop. After the legalization of Christianity, bishops acquired a civic status similar to that of important government officials and assumed the responsibility of managing large-scale charitable efforts."[28]

In his particular role as healer, the Christian bishop participated in a well-defined ministry with roots in the New Testament and guidelines in sources including the *Apostolic Tradition* and the *Canons of Hippolytus*. Ric Barrett-Lennard reminds his reader that the bishop, in his role as healer, would have overseen a structured ministry to the sick, identifiable in many cities of this period, containing three dimensions that all operated alongside one another: "ministry by the whole community to the sick, ministry by particular individuals with a charism for healing, and ministry to the sick by the leadership in the church."[29] The third canon of the *Canons of Hippolytus*, which formed part of the prayers recited during the episcopal consecration of many in fourth-century Egypt, reads, "Give him power to loosen every bond of the oppression of demons, to cure the sick and crush Satan under his feet quickly."[30] Again, Barrett-Lennard writes that in this petition, "the bishop himself is seen as a healer. . . . He is understood to be given a healing power in the course of his ordination as bishop. As a holy person and leader of the Christian community, the bishop is considered a man who is equipped by God to be a healer and to continue the healing work of Christ and the apostles."[31]

We may envision how such service, and the means of healing and reconciliation it may have afforded, was realized, received, and incorporated into the life of the individual Christian and in the life of the Christian community through an examination of evidence from the writings of Serapion of Thmuis. Unlike the evidence for Abba Ammonas, the extant writings of Abba Serapion were composed during Serapion's tenure as bishop and record some of the issues and concerns he confronted in that role. Moreover, we know of a strong relationship between Abba Antony and Abba Serapion that continued to exist after Abba Ammonas assumed leadership of this monastic network and Serapion was appointed bishop by Athanasius of Alexandria and oversaw administration of the local Christian community.

As a fellow monk, Serapion, like Ammonas, had received and exercised the gift of discernment in monastic and congregational contexts. The information we possess about the experiences of Serapion of Thmuis in this capacity provide a basis for considering how Abba Ammonas might have addressed some of the more salient issues Serapion raises, and how Abba Ammonas might have responded to Serapion's attempts to employ discernment as a means of unifying the members of his local Christian community with the members of the monastic network. During his time as a monastic leader, Serapion had acquired a relationship of mutual respect and support with Abba Antony, Abba Ammonas, and the other members of this monastic network. In his later years as an ecclesiastical leader, he would call for intercession and the exercise of discernment from this monastic network as he sought to unite his beleaguered community during the trinitarian debates of the mid-fourth century. While Serapion certainly sought to retain an alliance with Abba Ammonas and his monastic network for the purpose of combating local infiltrations of opposition to the claims of Nicea, his involvement in their lives rested primarily on his belief in the essential role of the exercise of discernment in the life of the Christian community.

In a letter written in 354 CE to the monk Dracontius, Archbishop Athanasius of Alexandria draws attention to the fact that Serapion, prior to appointment as bishop, had been a monk and a leader over a group of other monks.[32] As Claudia Rapp writes in her work, *Holy Bishops in Late Antiquity: The Nature of Christian Leadership in an Age of Transition,* "Athanasius was the first ecclesiastical leader to exploit the pool of monastic talent in a systematic way. He made it his policy to appoint monks to vacant bishoprics, knowing that he could depend on their loyalty in his struggle with Arians and Melitians."[33] Serapion's appointment as bishop positioned him in a lineage of formative Christian bishops. Located in the eastern Nile delta, Thmuis was one of the first Christian cities in Egypt. Eusebius' *Ecclesiastical History* makes special mention of Phileas, a bishop of Thmuis martyred under Emperor Diocletian, and his work on the martyrs of Alexandria, which shows early ties between this urban center and Thmuis.[34] The careers of others who held the episcopal seat of the city prior to Serapion attest further to the impact of martyrdom and schism on the region. At the time of the Council of Nicea, the seat was divided as the city claimed both a Melitian and an orthodox bishop. Serapion's writings indicate that his own episcopal career was marked by heavy involvement in the ecclesiastical and theological debates and dissension of his day and most likely ended with his exile. His *Letter to the Monks,* dated to the later decades of the fourth century, may have been issued after his episcopal service.

In his capacity as bishop, Serapion's conceptions of illness, health, and healing were informed, no doubt, by his monastic life, a life in which these figured prominently. As we have seen affirmed in the actions of Abba Ammonas, "healing played a central role in the emergence of monasticism in Egypt; holy men performed healing previously associated with Jesus and the apostles."[35] A statement about Serapion's own monastic formation and practice under Abba Antony is recorded in the *Life of Antony.*[36] Here, like Abba Ammonas, Serapion would have witnessed firsthand the techniques of prayer and blessing associated with what Andrew Crislip refers to as "the non-medical healing" of the monks in his experience as a disciple of Abba Antony.[37] Furthermore, Serapion remained a confidante to Antony well into his episcopal career, receiving descriptions of events from his former monastic guide.[38] The evidence of miracles and healings in the *Life of Antony* and similar accounts prompted Stanley Harakas to write that many "used the panoply of prayer together with their medical skills, folk wisdom, and herbal lore to cure the ills of others."[39]

That Serapion exercised those same techniques is possible; that he exercised the central gift of discernment, a gift of the Holy Spirit that lay at their core, is evident from passages in the *Apophthegmata Patrum* like the one that tells of a visit to Abba Serapion. When the abba counseled his visitor, a monk, to remain in his cell if he wished to make progress, his visitor was offended. Abba Serapion then said to him, "'Up to now you have called yourself a sinner and accused yourself of being unworthy to live, but when I admonished you lovingly, you were extremely put out. If you want to be humble, learn to bear generously what others unfairly inflict upon you and do not harbor empty words in your heart.' Hearing this, the brother asked the old man's forgiveness and went away greatly edified."[40] Another saying hearkens to the practice of humility and watchfulness, as it records Abba Serapion instructing: "When the soldiers of the emperor are standing at attention, they cannot look to the right or left; it is the same for the man who stands before God and looks towards him in fear at all times; he cannot then fear anything from the enemy."[41]

During his tenure as bishop, Serapion of Thmuis appears to have taken seriously the spirit of the charge in the third canon of the *Canons of Hippolytus* "to loosen every bond of the oppression of demons, to cure the sick and crush Satan under his feet quickly."[42] The prayers in the *Sacramentary of Serapion*, ascribed to the bishop and intended for use in public worship, provide evidence of the ministry to the sick by the whole community and by the leadership in the church. An examination of the *Letter on the Death of Antony*, a nonliturgical writing from Serapion written in the mid-fourth century affirms, perhaps not surprisingly, that healing was a recurring concern for the bishop and suggests ways in which ministry by particular individuals with a charism for healing may have functioned to complement the efforts of the bishop in this community.

The prayers that have come to us under the title *Sacramentary of Serapion* have received consistent attention for their historical and liturgical value. Maxwell Johnson concludes his extensive literary analysis of the prayers of Serapion of Thmuis by reminding that they "are a mid-fourth century Egyptian collection drawn from diverse sources which reflect different strata of historical, liturgical, and theological development."[43] Ric Barrett-Lennard's analysis of prayers for healing prominent in the *Sacramentary of Serapion* concludes that "the *Sacramentary of Sarapion*, and therefore the community or communities behind it, reflects a strong and consistent interest in matters of illness, health and healing."[44] While the intercessory prayers for the sick in the *Sacramentary of Serapion* request the alleviation from sickness, they do so in a way that honors and ensures the solidarity with the divine made possible by suffering. We see this, for example, in two prayers, Prayer 22 and Prayer 30. Using the categories for common prayers in this period identified by Matthias Klinghardt in his article, "Prayer Formularies for Public Recitation: Their Use and Function in Ancient Religion," Prayer 22 and Prayer 30 are best classified as homophonic response wherein "the prompter alone recites the entire prayer; the group does not repeat single lines of the formulary, but instead incorporates it as a common response in unison. Most common was the Amen response but there are a number of other examples, particularly in litanies."[45] Johnson, in support of the general position previously advanced by Louis Duchesne, has argued that within the *Sacramentary*, Prayer 22 and Prayer 30 belong with those "general prayers and blessings for various occasions (Prayers 19-30), probably including the proanaphoral section of the Eucharistic liturgy."[46] Directed by belief in the healing power of the divine, in Prayer 22, the "Prayer for the Sick,"[47] healing comes when the disease is rebuked when the lain body is raised.[48] The power for this is outside the human person. Appeal to the divine is appeal for an exercise of power, of control, over that which causes the illness. As creator of the soul, the divine is the source of rectification and restoration. An act of healing is perceived as an act of mercy. Here, suffering and sickness are viewed "in reference to its ultimate spiritual significance in the life of the individual afflicted."[49]

Such actions are upheld in another prayer, Prayer 30, which was probably used "in the church's specific ministry to the sick."[50] In Prayer

30, "Laying on of Hands of the Sick,"[51] as in Prayer 22, the dominant imagery is release from sickness; the origin and nature of the illness are secondary, since the emphasis is on the act of release. Release is required so that restoration can take place. Those actions of release that will make the sick well are accompanied in Prayer 30 by the call for an incorporation of divine power, in order to be healed through the name of Jesus Christ. It is telling that in several of his nonliturgical writings, Bishop Serapion would articulate a similar sentiment on behalf of the spiritual health of his community suffering from the sickness of their sin. In one of these writings, the *Letter on the Death of Antony*, he would expand notions of sickness, extend the ministry to the sick and continue to ensure the health of the Christian community.

An Ecclesial Context for Discernment

In his study of the *Letter on the Death of Antony*, Klaus Fitschen writes that the occasion for the letter was both the death of Antony and the occupation of the churches by the Arians.[52] What is clear is that Serapion's episcopal identity and rule, and his understanding of healing as well, is framed continuously by his alliance with those in the Antonian monastic network and by his alliance with his powerful and assertive archbishop. That Serapion could address these alliances simultaneously and for mutually beneficial ends is clear in the healing he hoped to proffer from his *Letter on the Death of Antony*. Authorship provided Serapion with an opportunity to extol his ascetic master and colleague and to call upon the intercessory prayer of his followers.

In the letter, Serapion laments that Antony's death has caused desolation and affliction precisely because he had served as an intercessor for the local churches: through his prayer, according to Serapion, Antony was able to prevent the descent of God's anger. Serapion draws on an analogy to the biblical figure, Aaron, in order to define both the severity of the current ecclesiastical crisis and the potency of the monk's response in terms of illness and healing.[53] His reference describes the reaction of the Israelites against the conditions of the wilderness and, in particular, the authority of Aaron and Moses recounted in Numbers 16. In the first uprising, two men and their families, Dathan and Abiram, rise up against Moses. The Lord appears and affirms Moses as the chosen leader; those who question the Lord are swallowed up by the earth. In the second uprising, the Levite Korah leads a rebellion of 250 people against Aaron, demanding a share of his priesthood. In an exercise of his authority, Moses steps in and tells Aaron, Korah, and his supporters to be prepared the following day to "present his censer before the LORD" (see Num 16:17). When all are assembled, the Lord appears in anger and threatens to consume the congregation of people, sparing only Moses and Aaron who beseech the Lord to act mercifully. "For wrath has gone out from the Lord, the plague has begun" (Num 16:46). Aaron then fills his censer, carries it to the congregation, and makes atonement for the people. "He stood between the dead and the living; and the plague was stopped" (Num 16:48).[54]

Serapion envisions the descent of divine anger in the current ecclesiastical crisis of similar proportion and the intercession of the monks as a necessary response. Just as Dathan, Abiram, Korah, and the others once angered the divine, so too the Arians and other Christians opposed to the Athanasian cause have done now. Just as Aaron and Moses once made atonement by their offering and prayer, so too Antony's followers must do now. Serapion makes this explicit by extending the intended parallel between the context and work of Aaron and those of Antony in containing the anger of the divine. Serapion appeals to the monks to serve as intercessors in Antony's stead.[55] Furthermore, the monks' solidarity with the crisis can be extended to Athanasius' plight as well since, through his prayer, Athanasius too appealed to them for assistance and solace.[56]

Serapion's analogy is informative. By it, he affirms that the intercession of these monks, like that of their predecessors, Moses and Aaron, is important to heal and restore the health of a sinful community before the divine. He invites the monks to participate in effecting a remedy, a medicine, for their sickness. As a result, Serapion uses the analogy to make the need for healing the illness of factionalism in his community a public concern. The distinction between desert and city, between rural and urban, is muted here because the sin is pervasive and affects all. Like the rebellions at the time of Moses and Aaron, the current crisis has angered the divine; it is grave and violent as it threatens to divide the community permanently. Furthermore, the connection between the illness of sin and the healing of prayer is centered in Serapion's identification with Moses, the "biblical model for bishops."[57] This identification allows Serapion to offer his invitation in the context of an authority that arises specifically from his roles of monk and bishop. If the illness is the product of collective sin, so too the healing is the product of a collective response. Serapion only emphasizes this when he reminds his audience that their prayers take place in solidarity with those of their archbishop, Athanasius.

Serapion's *Letter* emphasizes that the human cause of the spiritual sickness of the community, the sin of factionalism, causes the entire community to suffer as one body. To address the collective nature of the sickness, Bishop Serapion used alliances, rooted in relationships built on theological unity, to facilitate spiritual healing. As in the *Sacramentary*, intercession, in the form of corporate prayer, was a means of relieving suffering and making manifest the healing power of God. Serapion's appeals in the *Letter* to the members of the Antonian network for intercessory prayer, like his appeals to others in the community in the *Sacramentary*, were grounded in a relationship that honored a corporate role in and responsibility for the spiritual health of the entire community.

As "physician of the soul," Bishop Serapion maintained concern for the health of his community, a concern mirrored in the prayers and intercessions for the healing of sickness in both the *Sacramentary* and the *Letter on the Death of Antony*. As these works indicate, he accepted responsibility for the health of his community in a way that recognized both the health of the individual human body as a created being and the health of the body of the church as a collective witness to the power of that creation.[58] Serapion espoused the belief that his role in the diagnosis of sickness through the exercise of discernment, and the techniques of prayer and invocation applied, were means of participating in the healing activity of the divine. As in the *Sacramentary*, so too in the *Letter on the Death of Antony*, the exercise of the gift of discernment locates the "sickness" that is then offered to God, in prayer, for healing.[59]

Finally, as we have seen, the exchanges between Bishop Serapion and these Christian communities affirm that the health of the community is a collaborative responsibility. They define a specific relationship that is rooted in neither a dispensation of episcopal power nor a subordination to episcopal authority but, rather, in the belief that the healing power of the divine works through every member of the community.

Given Abba Ammonas' teachings about and examples of the exercise of discernment, Serapion of Thmuis' appeals to Abba Ammonas and to the other members of his monastic network after the death of Abba Antony would not have been merely the requests of a pained and desperate bishop. Rather, they would have been received as a promise of renewed solidarity. The monks' affirmative response to Serapion's appeals would have been an extension of hospitality to this community, thereby attesting to one of the ways this monastic network was functioning as praying intercessor in concert with the local bishop. Thus, the participation of Abba Ammonas and the members of this monastic network in this local community would have been a manifestation of a much more foundational bond.

Conclusion

Seeing it in the context of the trinitarian debates after Nicea, we understand better the relationship between Serapion of Thmuis with the community surrounding him and Abba Ammonas with his monastic network. Conflict had fueled internal processes of formalization whereby the Christian communities became more focused and centralized on statements of belief and on issues of organization. These processes received the support of Constantine and his sons who aided rather than opposed the rise of the authority of the bishop and provided resources for the expansion of the faith.

During their careers, Ammonas and Serapion were influential in the broader ecclesiastical concerns and debates among Christians in Egypt around the Nicene formula, produced at a council that was at the center of church-state relations in the early fourth century. In the words of Rowan Williams, "The record of the years that followed Nicea is one of monumentally complicated maneuvers to find another unifying formula."[60] Ongoing doctrinal dissension and controversy ensued.

The Nicene Creed was approved again in amplified form at the Council of Constantinople in 381 CE. One of the more obvious amplifications in this creedal formula regarded the nature and role of the Holy Spirit, "the most disputed area of belief towards the end of the Arian Controversy."[61]

In 325 CE, the creedal statement incorporated the claim to belief in the Holy Spirit. The theological debates in the latter half of the fourth century attested to the need for an explication of this claim. By 381 CE, this was achieved. In the Nicene-Constantinopolitan Creed, the relationship between the Son and the Holy Spirit is defined: the Son "was incarnate from the Holy Spirit and the Virgin Mary."[62] Likewise, there is expansion and qualification of the earlier expression in the Nicene Creed of belief in the Holy Spirit to address the relationship to the Father: "And in the Holy Spirit, the Lord the life giver, who proceeds from the Father, who with the Father and the Son is together worshipped and together glorified, who spoke through the prophets."[63]

It is a testament to early Christian communities throughout the empire that the development of their symbols was issued in both private and public expression, with particularity and universality. In this way, their efforts preserved the many dimensions of Christian spirituality. As we have seen and as the evidence for the relationship between Serapion of Thmuis and Ammonas suggests, in this period we might think of the relationship between the communal and personal dimensions of Christian spirituality as embodied symbolically by the bishop and the monk. As doctor of the church, the bishop was accountable for the exercise of discernment in the public life of the Christian community. In a similar way, but on a more personal level, as a physician of the soul the monk was accountable for the exercise of discernment in the private life of the Christian.

The spiritual father assisted others in their attempts to see and define and know a true relation to the divine as abba and guide. While the role of the spiritual father was essentially didactic, it was so in a broad, multifaceted sense. He embodied both the acquisition and the maintenance of the human-divine relationship. He was a living example of this relationship and of how it might exist in the world. He knew how to recover this relation and was able to help others do the same. His insight, and his ability to serve as intercessor, invited and empowered others to be part of a timeless community of righteousness rooted in love. As John Chryssavgis observes about the desert fathers and mothers, "The intensity of their struggle revealed the love for their neighbor as the integrity of their heart, and the love of God as the intention of their life. So it is not so much the great fast or the impressive feat that mattered in the desert but the principle of love."[64]

Validation, by those in the ministry and in the laity, of the experiences of Abba Ammonas and the members of his monastic network concretized and centralized discernment, the indwelling of the Holy Spirit, and the cultivation of received spiritual gifts in a way that extended baptismal belief in the hope and promise of new life in the resurrection. Because these spiritual fathers and mothers had experienced subsequent, postbaptismal, graces they attested to the continual presence of the Holy Spirit as teacher and as guide in the life of the individual Christian. In the midst of the clerical and doctrinal formalization of the late fourth century, these monks upheld the experience on which such formalization rested.[65] As a result, they lived a theology akin to what Vladimir Lossky defines as a trinitarian theology, "a theology of union, a mystical theology which appeals to experience, and which presupposes a continuous and progressive series of changes in created nature, a more and more intimate communion of the human person with the Holy Trinity."[66]

By legitimating Abba Ammonas' witness as an experience of the indwelling of the Holy Spirit, Serapion of Thmuis honored the role of discernment and its manifestation in the life of the local church community. The evidence of these relations between the ministry of the bishop and the stewardship of the monk, with the gift and exercise of discernment at its core, would have contributed to the expansion of Christianity in late antiquity. As Norman Russell writes:

> This development had theological repercussions. An intellectualist idea of faith came to be replaced by one that was more "institutionalized," the emphasis shifting from knowing God through the contemplation of the timeless cosmic order to encountering him through his historical revelation in Jesus Christ. The new emphasis

was accompanied by a suspicion of intellectuals, a focusing more on the shared experience of the community. The first abbas, with their teaching on self-knowledge and spiritual ascent hearkened back to an earlier world. From the episcopal point of view it was important that the abbas' authority and prestige should be harnessed to the ecclesiastical needs of the new era and that whatever seemed incompatible with those needs should be eliminated.[67]

As it continued to move beyond the boundaries of the empire governed by Constantine and his successors, Christianity would come to shed its Roman construction and emphasize itself as a faith accessible to all. Discernment would continue to serve as a cornerstone for the life of the Christian community because of its inclusion in the organization and structure of ministerial authority and in the celebration of rituals and sacraments accessible to all Christians. Yet, due to the efforts of Abba Ammonas and his monastic colleagues, discernment would now also be found in those physicians of the soul, those spiritual fathers and mothers whose lives stressed for others the choice of Christian discipleship as it was embedded in the indwelling of the Holy Spirit. By withdrawal from society, purification, restoration, and adoption, they were called to make sacred their bodies and souls and so to acquire union with the divine. Their spiritual formation required a surrender of the self in order to reestablish natural, original relations with the divine and so they offered a fundamental contribution to the life of the local Christian community.

In many ways, their monasticism served as "the expression under new conditions of the original evangelical concept of Christianity which had ruled the life of the early Church."[68] Their efforts ensured the preservation of a form of discernment, and the theological and pneumatological principles on which it rested, that may have been muted or lost in the processes of self-definition. Through their call to service these spiritual fathers and mothers situated their monasticism in the mainstream of the church, and so in a way made it integral to the church's development and formation. Thus, they contributed to the broader efforts of many Christians in this period to preserve an experience of discernment in conjunction with, rather than in opposition to, the institutionalized belief in the death and resurrection of Jesus Christ.

Jon Davies has written:

> The world of early Christianity was a cosmopolitan world, with a multiplicity of cultures and polities, some relatively new and inchoate, some relatively new and adamant. From such a world what would have seemed least likely at the time of the death of Christ must surely have been the conversion of the Roman Emperor and Empire to something called "Christianity" and the transformation of a small intra-Jewish argument into a major orthodoxy and dominant religious system of the Empire.[69]

The centrality of, and sustained access to, the gift of discernment in all of its forms and expressions would contribute to those processes of definition that characterized the transformation and development of Christianity in this period.

NOTES

1. Ammonas, *Ep. Syr.* 6; Chitty, *The Letters*, 7.
2. Ammonas, *Ep. Syr.* 12; Chitty, *The Letters*, 17.
3. Ammonas, *Ep. Syr.* 12; Chitty, *The Letters*, 16.
4. Ammonas, *Ep. Syr.* 12; Chitty, *The Letters*, 16.
5. Ammonas, *Ep. Syr.* 1; Chitty, *The Letters*, 1.
6. Ammonas, *AP* 8; Ward, 27; Ammonas, *AP* 8; Ward, 27.
7. Ammonas, *AP* 8; Ward, 27. See also Ammonas, *AP* 10; Ward, 28.
8. The *Didascalia Apostolorum* addresses the bishop as the one responsible for bringing healing to the community of the church (see *Didascalia Apostolorum* 2.20.11). It is also telling that the Syriac Codex of 534 CE contains the letters of Abba Ammonas and those of Nilus of Ancyra who had been called to leave monastic practice for the episcopal office. See Daniel Caner: "What emerges from Nilus' writings is a monastic world that was highly conditioned by concerns for material support and patronage. They also show that monks of his day were truly divided over the proper setting for monastic life: in cities among other people or in seclusion" (187).

9. See Stuart G. Hall, "Ministry, Worship and Christian Life," in Hazlett, *Early Christianity*, 101–11; here 101.

10. See Hall, 106. See also Victor Paul Furnish, *The Moral Teaching of Paul*: "If Christ's death is for Paul the decisive event by which God's love is established, then it is equally true that for Paul it is God's Holy Spirit that is the decisive bearer of God's love, the means by which God's love is made present in the believer's life" (25).

11. *The Didache* (*The Teaching of the Twelve Apostles*), 15.1-2; Michael W. Holmes, ed., *The Apostolic Fathers: Greek Texts and English Translations* (Grand Rapids, MI: Baker Books, 1999), 267. See Hall, 106.

12. Ignatius of Antioch, Letter to the Trallians, 2.1-2; Holmes, 160. See Hall, 106.

13. See *Didascalia Apostolorum* 2.25.7.

14. Henry Chadwick, *The Early Church*, 119. A highly practical tone is contained in the canons of the Synod of Elvira issued several decades after Cyprian's treatise. Some of these canons identify and treat the offices of bishop, presbyter, and deacon individually and collectively. There are clear prohibitions against sexual misconduct (Canon 18) as well as illicit business practices like usury and restriction of the duties of office holders (Canon 19 and Canon 20). See Hall, 106.

15. Noel King, "Church-State Relations," in Hazlett, *Early Christianity*, 244–55, here 249.

16. Peter Brown, *Power and Persuasion in Late Antiquity: Towards a Christian Empire* (Madison: University of Wisconsin Press, 1992), 76. See also Megan Hale Williams, *The Monk and the Book: Jerome and the Making of Christian Scholarship* (Chicago, IL: University of Chicago Press, 2006). On this transition under Emperor Constantine, Williams writes: "Under Constantine and his successors in the mid-fourth century, the decline of the urban elites in favor of a new administrative and military class accelerated. At the same time, the hierarchy of the Christian church began to take on the contours of an alternative civic leadership" (6).

17. *The Ecclesiastical History of Eusebius Pamphilus*, 9.2, trans. Christian Frederick Cruse (Grand Rapids, MI: Baker Book House, 1989), 404. See also Ramsay MacMullin, *Christianizing the Roman Empire (A.D. 100–400)*, 58. With regard to those drawn to the Christian community after 312 CE due to the impact of Constantine, MacMullin writes, "Thereby they played a causal part in the inclining of others to a slower, more serious conversion. Though too ignoble to have ensured any record, the change of heart that began out of mere imitation, fashion, and respectability must surely be assumed to have been at work in the great burst of growth that the church enjoyed after Constantine."

18. Bart Ehrman and Andrew Jacobs, eds., *Christianity in Late Antiquity, 300–450 CE: A Reader* (Oxford University Press, 2004), 129.

19. See Canon 4; Ehrman and Jacobs; reprinted from "Canons of Constantinople," in *The Church of the Ancient Councils: The Disciplinary Work of the First Four Ecumenical Councils,* ed. and trans. Peter L'Huillier (Crestwood, NY: St. Vladimir's Seminary Press, 1996).

20. See Canons 6, 7; Ehrman and Jacobs, *Christianity in Late Antiquity.*

21. See Canon 15; Ehrman and Jacobs, *Christianity in Late Antiquity.*

22. See Canons 10, 11, 12, 17; Ehrman and Jacobs, *Christianity in Late Antiquity.*

23. Canon 18; Ehrman and Jacobs, *Christianity in Late Antiquity.*

24. David Batson, *The Treasure Chest of the Early Christians: Faith, Care and Community from the Apostolic Age to Constantine the Great* (Grand Rapids, MI: Eerdmans Publishing Company, 2001), 109.

25. Henry Chadwick, "The Role of the Christian Bishop in Ancient Society," *Colloquy* 35 (Berkeley: Center for Hermeneutical Studies in Hellenistic and Modern Culture, 1979); reprinted in *Heresy and Orthodoxy in the Early Church* (London: Variorum Reprints, 1991).

26. Boniface Ramsey, *Beginning to Read the Fathers* (Mahwah, NJ: Paulist Press, 1985), 114. See also Clarence Gallagher, "The Imperial Ecclesiastical Lawgivers," in *The First Christian Theologians: An Introduction to Theology in the Early Church,* ed. G. R. Evans, 65–76 (Blackwell Publishing, 2004). Gallagher's observation reminds us that the rise of the bishop coincided with a preexisting conception of imperial authority: "The religious understanding of the emperor's role that had grown up in pagan imperial Rome did not disappear with the conversion of Constantine. The emperor continued to be regarded as the divinely appointed protector of the Church and the imperial power was expected to provide the Church with freedom and protection" (65).

27. Ric Barrett-Lennard, "The *Canons of Hippolytus* and Christian Concern with Illness, Health, and Healing," *Journal of Early Christian Studies* 13, no. 2 (2005): 139.

28. Darrel Amundsen and Gary Ferngren, "The Early Christian Tradition," in *Caring and Curing: Health and Medicine in the Western Religious Traditions,* ed. Ronald L. Numbers and Darrel W. Amundsen (New York: Macmillan, 1986), 48. These authors draw attention to the fact that disease or illness was attributed to one of three sources, namely, "God, demons, and nature." These were not necessarily mutually exclusive, as Amundsen and Ferngren write: "While Christians hesitated to attribute specific cases of illness directly to God, the more they stressed his sovereignty, the more they

saw him as the ultimate cause, regardless of whether the immediate cause was demonic or natural" (54).

29. Barrett-Lennard, 143.

30. Paul Bradshaw, ed., *The Canons of Hippolytus*, Alcuin/GROW Liturgical Study 2, Grove Liturgical Study 50 (Bramcote: Grove Books Limited, 1987), 12–13.

31. Barrett-Lennard, 152. Barrett-Lennard observes that the Christian bishop, in his particular role as healer, participated in a well-defined ministry with roots in the New Testament and guidelines in sources including the fourth-century *Canons of Hippolytus,* "a collection of thirty eight canons" that "represents an adaptation of the *Apostolic Tradition,*" of possibly Egyptian origin (139).

32. Athanasius of Alexandria, "Letter to Dracontius," PG 25: 523–34.

33. Claudia Rapp, *Holy Bishops in Late Antiquity: The Nature of Christian Leadership in an Age of Transition,* The Transformation of the Classical Heritage, XXXVII (University of California Press, 2005), 147.

34. *The Ecclesiastical History of Eusebius Pamphilus,* 8.10; Cruse, 329.

35. Amanda Porterfield, *Healing in the History of Christianity* (Oxford University Press, 2005), 48. Porterfield observes: "The preoccupation with sickness and death in early Christianity represented disconcerting tendencies towards individualism, as well as an enveloping sense of social and religious crisis that plagued Jews especially. For people drawn to Christianity, hopes of dispelling isolation, suffering, and fears of sickness and death coalesced around the person of Jesus and his victorious power of healing" (47).

36. See *Life of Antony,* 4 and 91. The fourth-century bishop, Serapion of Thmuis, was a proven ally both to Athanasius of Alexandria and to the desert ascetics; his letters betray his role as a liaison between the urban and desert communities. In addition, these letters show that his experiences as a former monastic leader were instrumental in shaping his understanding of the function and role of the episcopal office.

37. Andrew Crislip, *From Monastery to Hospital: Christian Monasticism and the Transformation of Health Care in Late Antiquity* (Ann Arbor: University of Michigan Press, 2005), 21. Such healing "draws exclusively on the perceived aid of a divine or quasi-divine agent" (21).

38. See *Life of Antony,* 82.

39. Stanley Harakas, "The Eastern Orthodox Tradition," Numbers and Amundsen, 151.

40. Serapion, *AP* 4; Ward, 227. This teaching is also enforced in Serapion, *AP* 1; Ward, 226.

41. Serapion, *AP* 3; Ward, 227.

42. "The Canons of Hippolytus," 132, Ehrman and Jacobs, 132.

43. Maxwell E. Johnson, *The Prayers of Sarapion of Thmuis: A Literary, Liturgical, and Theological Analysis* (Rome: Pontificio Instituto Orientale, 1995), 281. Like many other works from this period, debate also continues regarding attribution. Again, as Johnson concludes, "But is Sarapion himself then to be understood as the compiler and first editor of the entire collection? While the lack of explicit parallels in the authentic works of Sarapion does not permit me to conclude this with certainty, I can find no compelling reason not to accept this as a reasonable hypothesis" (283).

44. Ric Barrett-Lennard, *Christian Healing after the New Testament: Some Approaches to Illness and Healing in the Second, Third and Fourth Centuries* (Lanham, MD: University Press of America, 1994), 319.

45. Matthias Klinghardt, "Prayer Formularies for Public Recitation: Their Use and Function in Ancient Religion," *Numen* 46, no. 1 (1999): 20.

46. Johnson, *The Prayers of Sarapion of Thmuis*, 168.

47. Johnson, *The Prayers of Sarapion of Thmuis*, 73, 179–82.

48. Johnson observes that the petition to "rebuke" may be a reference to possession by demons or unclean spirits (Johnson, *The Prayers of Sarapion of Thmuis*, 181–82).

49. Amundsen and Ferngren, 46.

50. Johnson, *The Prayers of Sarapion of Thmuis*, 183.

51. Johnson, *The Prayers of Sarapion of Thmuis*, 81, 182–83.

52. Klaus Fitschen, *Serapion von Thmuis: Echte Und Unechte Schriften Sowie Die Texte Und Studien*, Patristische Texte und Studien 37 (Berlin and New York: Walter de Gruyter, 1992), 49. Attribution of the *Letter on the Death of Antony* is undisputed.

53. See Serapion of Thmuis, *Letter on the Death of Antony*, section 9 in Rene Draguet, *Une letter de Serapion de Thmuis aux disciples d'Antoine (A.D. 356) en versions syriaque et armenienne*, in *Le Museon* 64, (1951): 4–17.

54. See Serapion of Thmuis, *Letter on the Death of Antony*, 10.

55. See Serapion of Thmuis, *Letter on the Death of Antony*, 13.

56. See Serapion of Thmuis, *Letter on the Death of Antony*, 20.

57. See Rapp, 125.

58. There may be parallels here with the way in which, as Caroline Schroeder has shown in her book, *Monastic Bodies: Discipline and Salvation in Shenoute of Atripe* (Philadelphia: University of Pennsylvania Press, 2007), Shenoute develops the idea of the monastery as one corporate body in which sin is a disease (85).

59. It is interesting that Serapion may also have emphasized that the gravity of the ailment of sin supersedes that of physical illness in correspondence with his episcopal colleague, Eudoxius.

60. Rowan Williams, "Athanasius and the Arian Crisis," in *The First Christian Thelogians*, ed. G. R. Evans (Blackwell Publishing, 2004), 157–67, here 161.

61. Adolf M. Ritter, "Creeds," Hazlett, 98.

62. J. N. D. Kelly, ed., *Early Christian Creeds*, 3rd ed., (New York: Continuum, 2006), 297.

63. Kelly, 298. See Franz Dunzl, *A Brief History of the Trinity in the Early Church*, trans. John Bowden (New York: T & T Clark, 2007). With regard to this portion of the creed, Dunzl writes: "Here the divine dignity of the Holy Spirit is described with the term 'Lord' (which in Greek is put in the neuter, *to kyrion*, by analogy with *to pneuma*, something that cannot be expressed in English), and also with the Johannine statements that the Spirit gives life (John 6.63) and proceeds from the Father (John 15.26)" (125).

64. John Chryssavgis, "From Egypt to Palestine," 301.

65. Andrew Louth, "Mysticism," in Hazlett, 213: "Mystical theology, faithful to Nicene orthodoxy, manifests two features: first, an emphasis on the incarnation as bridging the gulf between Creator and creature, and secondly, a deepening insistence on the fundamental unknowability of God."

66. Vladimir Lossky, *The Mystical Theology of the Eastern Church* (Crestwood, NY: St. Vladimir's Seminary Press, 1976), 67.

67. Norman Russell, "Bishops and Charismatics in Early Christian Egypt," in Behr, Louth, and Conomos, 100.

68. Alexander Schmemann, *Historical Road of Eastern Orthodoxy* (Crestwood, NY: St. Vladimir's Seminary Press, 1977), 106. See also Lawrence Cunningham, "*Extra Arcam Noe*: Criteria for Christian Spirituality," in *Minding the Spirit: The Study of Christian Spirituality*, ed. Elizabeth A. Dreyer and Mark S. Burrows, 171–78 (Baltimore, MD: Johns Hopkins University Press, 2005). Cunningham writes of the connection to tradition: "The historical tradition of Christianity, shaped by creed, ethos, and worship, is both circumscribed and elastic. It has a definite shape, but it is a shape that is in process and not finished" (175).

69. Jon Davies, *Death, Burial and Rebirth in the Religions of Antiquity* (London and New York: Routledge, 1999), 17.

Monasticism, Mysticism, and Ecclesia

There are many things that I want to write to you. But these few I have written because of the great love that I have for you. Farewell in your heart, in our Lord, in every act of love for God.[1]

Abba Ammonas' commission to this audience was ripe with a promise of hope. This is noteworthy given that his words were issued during a time of controversy and transition, a time that bore witness to the shifting shape and scope of Christian ecclesiology. His contribution to the processes of self-definition that marked the church of his day rested in his conviction that the gift of discernment was for the life of the entire Christian community.

Given the evidence that we have explored, we return to imagine briefly the reception of this gift from a final perspective, namely, that of a member of this community who might have first learned of Abba Ammonas through the stories recounted by fellow Christians who had traveled to the desert seeking Ammonas' counsel and intercession. In her daily conversations and prayer with her fellow Christians, our Christian would have heard about personal encounters with this desert monk, this solitary one, and about his earnest struggle to take refuge in a deep awareness of the divine as the source and sustenance of his being. Through these stories, she might have been afforded a glimpse of the role of the divine in the life of Abba Ammonas, and through the descriptions of his monastic practice she would have been provided a lens for envisioning his training for self-knowledge and knowledge of his place before the divine. She might have learned, too, about Abba Ammonas' emphasis on the experience of the Holy Spirit, on the need to cultivate withdrawal, solitude, quiet, and prayer, and on the ascent of the soul, and so about how discernment was acquired and how it might function in private and public expression as a means of helping others to respond rightly to the challenge of Christian discipleship.

Sustained by these stories and descriptions, and desirous of the healing affected through Abba Ammonas' cultivation of the gift of discernment, our Christian might then have made the journey to visit him. Like many previous pilgrims to Abba Ammonas, she might have asked him to guide her in prayer, to counsel her about a specific problem, to advise her about a pressing decision in her spiritual life or to recommend a course for future action. She may have sought a faith healing, asking Ammonas to lay his hands on her or touch her with a sacred object. Regardless of the particular issue, she would have maintained a willingness to see divine intervention through Abba Ammonas' virtue and holiness, and she would have realized that it was through his fundamental union with all Christians that his vocation to serve the members of her local community as intercessor was a distinctively ecclesiastical one. She would have understood that his involvement in the world—and, in particular, in her world—contributed to and was in constant solidarity with the life of her local Christian community.

Our Christian would have returned from her visit with a renewed awareness of the way in which her call to Christian discipleship was intimately tied to that of Abba Ammonas' and to the liturgical life of the church because of her belief that the indwelling of the Holy Spirit instilled a desire for deeper union with the divine. She might incorporate his teaching into her daily life; she might continue to strive for a life of holiness and spiritual vigor in renewed solidarity with others trying to live holy and exemplary lives on this earth.

After several months, our Christian might decide to seek again the counsel of Abba Ammonas and return to the desert. Unable to locate him, she would inquire after his whereabouts. In response, she would be told that he had left the desert to assume an episcopal appointment because his discernment made him particularly suited to service in a position of ecclesiastical leadership.[2] One of the stories circulating about Abba Ammonas would have confirmed that his commissioning was a product of this spiritual gift.[3] Our Christian would have recognized that Abba Ammonas' actions were indicative of the expansive capacity of the exercise of discernment. In the course of conversations, our Christian may have heard of other monks who had been called in a similar way to leave their monastic practice for the episcopal office.

Our Christian might also be told about Bishop Ammonas' continued involvement in the life of the monastic network he left and, in particular, about two recent letters the monks had received from him. In one letter, he reminded them to remain steadfast during trials and to exercise obedience, instructing them, "both in this and in other matters, hearken to your teachers so that you make progress."[4] In the other letter, he exhorted a spiritual father directly: "But do you, as a good teacher, take earnest care of those in your charge, and perhaps it will please God to bring you out from this tabernacle, leaving behind you a good seed. We know that you are an excellent teacher and educator. But remember that it is for the sake of this seed that God has left you in this tabernacle."[5]

In all of this, our Christian would have realized that it was precisely because others acknowledged Abba Ammonas' activity as a testimony to the constant breath of the Holy Spirit in the life of the Christian community that his contribution was a valued one. Because he was recognized as having experienced subsequent, postbaptismal, graces his life attested to the continual presence of the Holy Spirit as teacher and as guide in the life of the individual Christian and in the shared life of the community. In the midst of the clerical and doctrinal formalization of the late fourth century, Ammonas' life held up as an example the experience on which such formalization rested. His acquisition of the gift of discernment allowed him to see in a way that was critical and necessary for others in this period; as a result, his vision contributed directly to the formation and development of a distinctly Christian worldview.

NOTES

1. Ammonas, *Ep. Syr.* 2; Chitty, *The Letters*, 3.

2. Abba Ammonas may have been consecrated bishop at some point although there is no recollection or record in the ecclesiastical lists.

3. Ammonas, *AP* 8; Ward, 27.

4. Ammonas, *Ep. Syr.* 9; Chitty, *The Letters*, 11. With regard to this letter and the next letter, Nau suggests the possibility that Abba Ammonas had left the community at the time of writing without further explanation of his status. In order to treat those references to his assumption of the episcopal office, I am exploring the possibility that these were written in that capacity.

5. Ammonas, *Ep. Syr.* 13; Chitty, *The Letters*, 20.

Part Two

The Writings
of Abba Ammonas[1]

Translated by

Nada Conic and Br. Lawrence Morey, OCSO
(The Letters, the Four Teachings, the Discourse to Solitaries,
the Instructions to Novices, and the two Fragments)

and by

Richard Upsher Smith, Jr.
(The Exhortations, or Paragraphs of Encouragement)

---

1. Francois Nau, "Ammonas, successeur de Saint Antoine," *Patrologia Orientalis* 11, 1915, 432–87. Letters 1–7 are given on pages 432–54; the Instructions or Teachings are given on pages 455–58; the Exhortations, or Paragraphs of Encouragement, are given on pages 458–71. The Discourse to Solitaries is on pages 472–74; and the Instructions for Novices are given on pages 474–84. The two Fragments are on pages 484–87. The critical text of Letter 8 is found in G.L. Marriott, *Macarii Anecdota: Seven Unpublished Homilies of Macarius* (New York: Harvard University Press,1969), 47–48, where it is labeled as the seventh homily.

LETTERS OF ABBA AMMONAS

The *Letters* of Abba Ammonas are evidence of the fluidity of relations and of ideas among Egyptian desert monks of the mid- and late fourth century. These letters attest to Abba Ammonas' affiliation with Abba Antony, to the mystical tradition that developed with the codification of monastic practice in this period, to the nature of spiritual formation in monastic practice, and to an understanding of that practice as a form of Christian discipleship.

B. M. Z.

Letter 1

FROM OUR HOLY AND INSPIRED ABBOT AMMONAS

On the Practice of Silence

You too know, my beloved brothers, that from the time the transgression[1] happened, the soul has not been able, as it should, to recognize God, unless it withdraws itself from people and from all distraction. Then it will see the attack of those fighting against it. If it should win the battle which comes to it at times, then the spirit of God will dwell within it, and all its labor will be transformed into joy and happiness. During these battles, sadness, *acedia*, and various burdens assault the soul, but let it not be afraid. They will not overcome the soul while it walks in the practice of stillness.[2]

Our holy fathers, too, withdrew into the deserts, Elijah the Tishbite, John the Baptist, and the other fathers.[3] Do not think that

---

1. παράβασις (*parabasis*). Ammonas is probably referring to the sin of Adam, following Rom 5:14 and 1 Tim 2:14.

2. "practice of stillness" = ἡσυχία, a fairly broad term, literally meaning "silence," but inferring tranquility, stillness, and rest and perhaps inferring withdrawal (see the discussion in G. W. Lampe, *A Patristic Greek Lexicon* [New York: Oxford University Press, 1961]).

3. Saint Jerome was acquainted with the idea that attributed the origins of monastic life to Elias and John the Baptist. He wrote to this effect at the beginning of the *Life of St. Paul of Thebes*: "Some, going back further, suppose that the beginning

those who are just who live among other people have accomplished their justification in the midst of them. No, having practiced a great deal of stillness first, they held fast a holy power dwelling within them. Then, when they possessed the virtues, God sent them into the midst of people, so they might become edifiers of people and heal their weaknesses. They were doctors of the soul and were able to heal weaknesses. Because of this ability, they were torn away from their peaceful solitude[4] and were sent out to people. But God sends them only after he has healed them from all their own illnesses. It is impossible that God should send a soul into the midst of people for their edification when it still has weaknesses. Those who leave before they have been perfected go by their own will, and not by the will of God. For God says regarding such people, "I did not send them out, but they ran of themselves."[5] Because of this, they can neither guard themselves nor edify others.

Those whom God sends do not wish to depart from their solitude[6] knowing that because of it they possessed divine powers. Nevertheless in order not to disobey the Creator they do leave, for the edification of the people.

[of monastic life] is from Blessed Elias and John." See also the beginning of the *Life of Pachomius*, PL 73. (For a modern edition of the *Life of St. Paul* see Pierre Leclerc, trans., *Jérôme: Trois Vies de Moines*, Sources Chrétiennes, vol. 508 [Paris: Cerf, 2007]. This passage is found on p. 144 of that volume. A translation is available in Roy J. Defarrari, ed., *Early Christian Biographies*, Fathers of the Church, vol. 15 [New York: Fathers of the Church, 1952], with our passage on p. 225. A translation of *The Life of Pachomius* is available in Armand Veilleux, trans., *Pachomian Koinonia*, vol. 1, CS 45 [Kalamazoo, MI: Cistercian, 1980]. The various modern editions are cited there. The passage in question is found on p. 24 and 298.)

4. ἡσυχία.

5. Jer 23:21. The reference from Jer 23:21 in the Septuagint text available to us reads, οὐκ ἀπέστελλον τούς προφήτας καὶ αὐτοὶ ἔτρεχον οὐκ ἐλάλησα πρὸς αὐτοὺς καὶ αὐτοὶ ἐπροφήτευον, or "I did not send the prophets but they ran, I did not speak to them but they prophesied."

6. ἡσυχία.

I made you understand, then, the power of the practice of stillness, and God approves of this power. Since you have learned the great benefit and value of this practice of stillness, you will attain it.

Most monks have not attained this stillness because they have remained with people. On account of this, they could not win out entirely over their own will. They did not want to subdue themselves so as to flee from the distraction of human company, but remained distracted with them. Therefore they did not learn the sweetness of God, they were not accounted worthy that the power of God should dwell in them or that they should have a share in themselves of the divine quality. The power of God, then, does not dwell in them since they distract themselves with the things of this world, and they are driven by the passions of the soul and by human opinions and the wishes of the old man.[7]

From the foundation of our tradition God fulfilled for us what is to come. Be strengthened, then, in what you do. Those who turn away from the practice of stillness are not able to defeat their own will, nor can they win the wrestling match being waged against them. Because of this, they do not have the power of God living within them, for it does not dwell in those enslaved to the passions. But as for you, vanquish the passions and the power of God will come all by itself into you.

---

7. Paul's "old man," as at Rom 6:6; Eph 4:22; and Col 3:9.

Letter 2

FROM THE SAME

Regarding the Cultivation of Grace

To the beloved in the Lord, greetings.

If you love the Lord with all your heart, with all your soul, and with all your might[1] remain in fear, fear will beget weeping, weeping joy, and joy will beget strength, and through this strength the soul will bear fruit in all things. And if God sees that this fruit of the soul is so ripe, He will receive it as a sweet smell, and in everything He, along with His angels, will rejoice with the soul, and will give it a guard to keep it in all its ways[2] so that he may guide it into a place of rest, and Satan may not overpower it. As often as the devil sees this guard, which is the force encircling the soul, he flees, afraid to approach, wary of the power surrounding it. Because of this, I know that you, beloved in the Lord, whom my soul loves, are lovers of God. Hold this force, then, inside yourselves, so that Satan may fear you, so that you may be wise in all your works, and so that the sweetness of grace may progress and increase its fruit in you. For the sweetness of the spiritual gift[3] is sweet—"more

---

1. Matt 22:37; Deut 6:5; etc.
2. Ps 90:11.
3. Rom 1:11.

than honey and the honeycomb."[4] Most monks and virgins have not known the great sweetness of this grace, since they did not acquire the heavenly force, except perhaps a few here and there. Nor did they cultivate this force, and because of this the Lord did not give it to them. For to those who cultivate it, God gives it, for he is no respecter of persons,[5] but to those who cultivate it, he gives it, from generation to generation.[6]

So now beloved, I know that you are lovers of God, and, from the time you took up this work, that you have loved God with your whole heart. I too, therefore, love you with my whole heart, because of the righteousness of your hearts. Acquire then for yourselves this divine force, so that you may pass all your time in freedom, and so that the work of God may be easy for you. This is the force given here to human beings, which leads them back into that rest, until they move beyond every "power of the air."[7] For there are energies in the air which hinder people, which do not want to release them to go to God. Let us pray earnestly, therefore, to God, so that they may not hinder us going to Him. As long as those who are just have the divine force with them, nothing can hinder them. And this is how we cultivate this force, until finally it dwells in us. We disdain every injustice and all honors, and hate every advantage of this world, those advantages considered valuable. We hate, too, all bodily rest, and cleanse the heart from all base thought and from all vain worry of this age, and so pray in fasting and tears night and day. Then the good God will not delay in giving this power to you. And when he does give it to you, you will continue through your time here in rest and ease. You will find great boldness in the presence of God, and then he will grant you all your prayers,[8] as it is written.

4. Ps 18:11; Ps 118:103; Sir 24:10.
5. Acts 10:34.
6. Ps 32:11; Luke 1:50; and many other places.
7. Eph 2:2.
8. Ps 36:4.

However, if the divine heat leaves and deserts you after you have received it, seek it again and it will come. This is God's heat, so it is like fire which changes coldness into its own fuel. And if you see your own heart becoming heavy at certain times, bring your soul before you and examine it with reverent thought, according to right reason. Then by necessity it will again grow warm and burn in God. So too the prophet David, when he saw his heart grow heavy, said, "I poured out my soul in me."[9] "I remembered the days of old, and I meditated on all your works,"[10] and what follows. He made his own heart grow warm again, and received the sweetness of the all-holy Spirit.

9. Ps 41:5.
10. Ps 142:5.

Letter 3

FROM THE HOLY ONE

Concerning Clear-Sighted Grace and Preserving Ourselves from Careless Ones

To my beloved brothers in Christ, greetings.

You know that I write to you as my beloved children, and children of the promise,[1] and children of the kingdom. Because of this I remember you night and day[2] so that God may guard you from every evil and that you may ask and ponder continually how he might grant you discretion and clear sight so that you might learn to discern the difference between good and evil in all things. For it is written: "Strong food is for the perfect, those who through habit have trained their senses for the discernment of good and evil."[3] These are they who have become the children of the kingdom.[4] They are reckoned among the number of the adopted,[5] those to whom God has given this clear sight in all their works, so that no one may lead them astray. For one may be trapped by the pretext

---

1. See Gal 4:28.
2. See 2 Tim 1:3.
3. Heb 5:14.
4. Matt 8:12; 13:38.
5. See Rom 8:15.

of good, and many are thus led astray, since they have not received from God this clear sight. This is why the blessed Paul, knowing that this clear sight is the great wealth of the faithful, said, "Because I bend my knees night and day before our Lord Jesus Christ for you, so that he may give you the revelation in his knowledge, enlightening the eyes of your heart so that you might know what is the breadth and the length and the height and the depth, and that you might know the overflowing love of the knowledge of the Lord,"[6] and what follows. Since Paul loved them with his whole heart, he wished the great wealth which he knew, that is, clear-sightedness in Christ, to be given to his children whom he loved. He knew that, if it were given to them, they would no longer grow weary in any labor, nor would they be tormented by any terror. Instead, the joy of God would be with them night and day and the work of God would be sweet to them, "more than honey and the honeycomb."[7] God would be with them through everything, and he would give them revelations and great mysteries which I am not able to articulate.

So now, beloved, since you are counted as children to me pray night and day in zeal and in faith and in tears so that you may attain this clear-sightedness, this gift which indeed you have not yet attained[8] since you came to this ascetic practice. And I, lowly as I am, pray on your behalf so that you may arrive at this progress and maturity to which not many of the monks have come, except a few rare and God-loving souls here and there. And if you wish to come to this measure, do not habitually spend time with monks of the careless sort among you, but keep yourselves from them; otherwise they do not allow you to progress in the things of God, but extinguish your fervor. For those who are careless do not have fervor but follow their own wills. If they meet you and talk about the things of this world, because of their company they

---

6. Eph 3:14-19, conflated with Eph 1:16-19.
7. Ps 18:11.
8. Phil 3:13.

extinguish and remove from you your fervor, and do not allow you to advance. As it is written, "Do not extinguish the spirit."[9] But the spirit is extinguished by vain speech and by distraction. When you see such people, act well toward them and flee from them and do not mix with them. It is they who do not allow anyone to progress in these times.

Farewell in the Lord, beloved, in the spirit of humility.

9. 1 Thess 5:19.

Letter 4

Concerning the trials which happen to those advancing on the way to God, that trials procure profit for them and that it is not possible that the soul should progress or make its way up toward God apart from trials.

I know that you are heartbroken, stricken with trials,[1] but if you endure nobly, you will possess joy. If trials do not come to you, either openly or in secret, you cannot receive aid above what you are used to receiving. All the saints were found in trials when they asked that their faith be increased. For whenever anyone receives a blessing from God a trial from the enemies is immediately added. They wish to deprive him of the blessing with which God has blessed him. The *daimons*, therefore, when they know that the soul which has been blessed receives advancement, wrestle openly or in secret against it. When Jacob was blessed by his father, for example, the trial of Esau immediately fell upon him.[2] The devil moved Esau's heart against Jacob, wishing to nullify the blessing. But he has no power against the just, for it is written: "The Lord will not let the rod of the sinners rest upon the inheritance of the

1. Jas 1:2.
2. Gen 27.

just."[3] So Jacob did not lose the blessing which he received, but increased it day by day. You too, then, work hard to become better through trials, for those who have obtained blessing must, by necessity, endure trials as well. Even I, your father, have endured great trials, both in secret and in the open, but accepting and begging for the will of God, I endured, and he brought me safely through.[4]

You too, then, my beloved, because God's blessing fell upon you, trials followed. Endure them until you get beyond them. For if you get beyond them you will obtain great success and increase in all your virtues, and a great joy which you have not yet known will be given to you from heaven. The remedy for overcoming trials is that you not be neglectful, but pray to God giving thanks with your whole heart and persevere in everything, and they will pass from you. For Abraham too, and Jacob, and Job, and many others were tried and turned out more worthy. As it is written, "Many are the troubles of the just, and the Lord rescues them from them all."[5] And again James says: "Anyone who is discouraged among you, let that one pray."[6] Do you see how all the saints, when they fell into times of trial, called upon God?

Again it is written: "God is faithful, and he will not allow you to be tried beyond your strength."[7] For that very reason, through the uprightness of your hearts God will work with you. If he did not love you, he would not lay trials upon you. For it is written, "The one whom the Lord loves, he disciplines, he chastises the child whom he receives."[8] And so the condition of trials is laid upon the faithful, but those who are untried are illegitimate children.[9] While they wear monastic clothing, they deny its power. Antony

---

3. Ps 124:3.
4. Gen 35:3—continuing the reference to the story of Jacob and Esau.
5. Ps 33:20.
6. Jas 5:13 ἀθυμεῖ τις ἐν ὑμῖν, προσευχέσθω— our text reads καταπάθει τις ἐν ὑμῖν, προσευχέσθω.
7. 1 Cor 10:13.
8. Prov 3:12. See Heb 12:6.
9. Heb 12:8.

said to you that no one can enter the kingdom of God who has not been tested.[10] And the apostle Peter says, "In this you rejoice, if it is necessary to be saddened by various trials, so that the genuineness of your faith, much more honorable than perishable gold, might be found through the fire of testing."[11] They say that trees root themselves more firmly and grow taller when they are shaken by winds. In this, then, and in other things, listen to your teachers so that you will make progress.

Know that, when it comes to spiritual work, the Spirit provides joy at the beginning [for the just], seeing that their hearts are pure. But when the Spirit has given them joy and sweetness, then it flees and abandons them. This is its sign. And it does this in the beginning with every soul which seeks God. It flees and abandons them, so that it knows if they seek God or not. Some, when the Spirit flees and overthrows them, endure oppression and they sit unmoving in their heaviness. They do not pray to God that he may remove the oppression so that joy and sweetness might come to them, that joy and sweetness which they once knew. But through their carelessness even their own wills are made strangers to the sweetness of God. Because of this, they become carnal.[12] They only wear the monastic habit, but have denied its power. They are those who are blind in their own lives and do not know the work of God.

If, however, they become aware of an oppression contrary to what they are used to and to their previous joy, and they beg God with tears and fasting, then the good God, if he sees that they ask in uprightness and with their whole heart and that they deny their own will entirely, gives them greater joy than before, and

---

10. PG 65: 77. (Jean-Claude Guy, ed. and trans., *Aphophthegmata Patrum,* Sources Chrétiennes 387, 474, 498 [Paris: Cerf, 1993, 2003, 2005], is the systematic collection, which does not include this particular saying [Antony *AP* 5]. PG is still the only available source. There is an English translation in Benedicta Ward, trans., *The Sayings of the Desert Fathers: The Alphabetical Collection,* CS 59 [Kalamazoo: Cistercian, 1975].)

11. 1 Pet 1:6-7.

12. See 1 Cor 3:3.

establishes them more firmly. This is the sign which he gives to every soul seeking God.

When the soul is lifted out of Hades, as far as it follows the Spirit of God, so far are trials imposed upon it in various places.[13] Moving past these trials, the soul becomes clear-sighted and takes on a new dignity. When Elias was about to be taken up, when he came to the first heaven, he was astounded at its brightness. But when he went up to the second heaven, he was so astounded that he said, "I considered the brightness of the first heaven as darkness." And so it was for each single heaven of the heavens.[14] The souls of the perfectly just, then, advance and rise up until they arrive at the final heaven.

I write these things to you, beloved, so that you may be made firm and learn that trials come to the faithful, not as a penalty, but for your gain, and unless trials come to the soul, it is not able to mount up to the place of the One who made it.[15] If you wish to receive spiritual grace then prepare yourselves for bodily hardships, and hardships of the heart. Stretch your thoughts up to heaven day and night, praying to the Spirit of fire[16] with your whole heart, and grace will be given to you.

See that wavering thoughts never enter your heart, saying to you: "Who can receive this?" Do not allow these thoughts to get hold of you, but pray in uprightness and you will receive [this spiritual grace]. And I, your Father, pray that you may receive it.

---

13. "lifted out"— ἀναφέρεται; "imposed upon"— ἐπιφέρονται; ". . . in various places"—see Matt 24:7 and parallels.

14. Nau, 445, sees an allusion to *Ascension of Isaiah*, 8.2. But the similarity is vague. See instead *Ascension of Isaiah* 8:1, 24–25; M. A. Knibb, trans., *Ascension of Isaiah: Martyrdom and Ascension of Isaiah*, 8:1, 24–5, *The Old Testament Pseudepigrapha*, ed. James H. Charlesworth (Garden City: Doubleday, 1985), 168–69.

15. The Greek at this point switches from Syriac letter 10 to letter 8.

16. May be a reference to 1 Kgs 18:21-40. See Antony Letter 6.73-75; Samuel Rubenson, *Letters of St. Anthony: Monasticism and the Making of a Saint* (Minneapolis, MN: Fortress, 1995), 221.

For the one who cultivates it continually[17] will receive it. That Spirit dwells among those who are upright of heart. And I am your witness that with uprightness of heart you do seek God. When you receive this Spirit, it will reveal to you the mysteries of heaven. It will reveal many things which I cannot write down. So you will not be afraid, free from every fear, and the joy of heaven will set you apart. You will be as though already transferred to the kingdom while still in the body. No longer will you need to pray for yourselves, but only for others.

Glory be to the good God, to the one who deems the servants known to him worthy of such mysteries, to him glory is fitting forever. Amen.

---

17. κατὰ γενεὰν καὶ γενεάν, lit. "from generation to generation," which we have generalized, since, while the biblical phrase may have been familiar in this context to Ammonas' readers, it is confusing in English.

Letter 5

That it is difficult to know the will of God, and that unless people deny their own will entirely and heed those who are their parents according to the spirit they will not be able to know the will of God or to make spiritual progress.

You know, my brothers, that when people's lives have changed and they come into another life, pleasing to God and better than the former, their names are also changed. So when our holy Forebears advanced [in holiness], what they were called also was changed, and a new name was applied to them, one written on the tablets of heaven. When Sarai made progress, it was said to her, "Your name will no longer be called Sarai, but Sarah."[1] Abram was called Abraham, and Isak, Isaac, and Jacob, Israel; and Saul's name was changed to Paul, and Simon's to Cephas, since their lives had changed and they had advanced beyond what they were. Because of this, since you have gained in your stature according to God, you also must change your name from your advancement according to God.

And so, beloved in Christ, whom I love with my whole heart, and whose advantage I seek as my own, since you have been reckoned as children to me according to God, I hear that trials oppress

---

1. Gen 17:15.

you, and I am afraid that the cause lies with you. For I heard that you wish to leave your place [in the desert], and I was saddened, even though I have not been overcome by sadness for a long time. For I know very clearly that if you abandon your place you will not make any progress whatsoever, for this is not at all the will of God. If you go away of your own accord, God will not aid you, nor will he go out with you, and I'm afraid that we will fall into a multitude of evils. If we follow our own will, God will no longer send us his power which gives success to all the ways of people. For if people perform some deed of their own accord, God will not aid them, and their hearts will grow bitter and powerless in everything they turn to. The deception of the faithful and their mockery, then, comes under the cover of advancement. By no other means was Eve led astray than by the pretence of good and of advancement, having heard that "you will be as gods."[2] Not discerning the voice of the one speaking to her, she did not heed God's command, and, far from encountering good, fell under a curse.

Solomon says in Proverbs, "There are roads which seem good to people, but their end leads to the depth of Hades."[3] He says this about those people who do not understand the will of God, but follow their own will. Not perceiving the will of God, they receive at first a fervor from the devil, which is like joy, but which is not joy. And later, the demon gives them gloominess and humiliation. But the one following the will of God endures great trouble in the beginning and later finds rest and rejoicing. So do nothing until I meet with you.

There are three [separate] wills which are the constant companions of a person. And many monks are ignorant of them, with the exception of those who are perfect, about whom the Apostle says: "Strong food is for the perfect, those whose senses have been trained through habit to discern good and evil."[4] And what are

---

2. Gen 3:5.
3. Prov 16:25. Our text differs slightly.
4. Heb 5:14.

these three wills? That which is insinuated by the enemy, that which is born in the heart, and that which is sown by God in a person. But of these, God accepts only that which is his own.

Test yourselves, therefore, [to see] which of the three wills drives you to leave your place. Do not leave until I can meet with you, just as [Jesus] says in the Gospel, "Remain in Jerusalem until you receive power from on high."[5] For I know the will of God for you in this case better than you do. It is difficult to recognize what the will of God is all the time. Unless people deny their own will entirely, and heed those who are their parents according to the spirit, they will not be able to recognize the will of God. When they do recognize it, then they seek power from God, so that they may be strong enough to do his will.

To recognize the will of God, therefore, is a great accomplishment, but to do it is greater still. Jacob possessed these powers when he obeyed his parents. For once they had told him to go away to Laban in Mesopotamia he readily obeyed, although he did not wish to be separated from his parents. But because he obeyed, he inherited the blessing.[6] And unless I, who am your father, had obeyed my [own] spiritual parents, God would not have revealed his will to me. Now you likewise must listen to your father in this matter, so that you might find rest and progress.

I heard that you have said that your father is ignorant of your distress.[7] We know that Jacob fled from Esau, but he did not run away of his own accord. He was sent away by his parents. Imitate Jacob, therefore, and remain until your father sends you away. Then you depart with a blessing, and God will approve all your affairs.

Farewell in the Lord. Amen.

5. Luke 24:49, paraphrased.
6. See Gen 27–28.
7. Nau remarks, "This whole letter shows that Ammonas had left the monastery" (449n3).

Letter 6

From your father among the saints Abba Ammonas

A word regarding pleasing people[1] and vainglory.

To my most honored brethren in the Lord, greetings.

I write to you as to the most beloved of God, and as those who seek the Lord in truth and with your whole hearts. God will heed such people when they pray and will bless them in everything and grant all the prayers of their soul whenever they call on him. But those who come to him with less than their whole heart, with two minds, those who do their works so that they receive the good opinion of others, these will not be heeded by God in what they ask of him. Instead he is angered by their works, for it is written that, "God scattered the bones of those who please other people."[2]

You see how God is angered by the works of such people and grants them none of the prayers which they ask from him, but instead even opposes them. This is because they do not do their works in faith, but according to human standards. Therefore divine power does not dwell in them and they are defective in every work which they undertake. Therefore they do not know the power of grace, nor its lightness, nor its joy. Instead, their souls are weighed

---

1. See Eph 6:6-7; and Col 3:22-23.
2. Ps 52:6.

down, burdened by all of their works. The majority of monks are like this. They did not receive the power of grace, that power which approves the soul, prepares it to rejoice, day after day provides it with good cheer, and warms their souls in God. For they do their works according to human standards. As a result, grace did not visit them. A person doing works to please other people is repugnant to the power of God.

You, my beloved, whose fruit has been reckoned in God, strive then in all your works, watchful of the spirit of vainglory, so that you may be victorious over it in everything, and so that all of your fruit may be acceptable and remain alive in the presence of the Creator, and so that you may receive the power of grace which is stronger than all these things. I am convinced regarding you, brothers, that whatever is possible for you to this end, you do it fighting against the spirit of vainglory. Struggle against it always. Because of this [struggle], your fruit lives. For this evil spirit comes with every righteous act to which one applies oneself, wanting to scatter its fruit and make it useless, in order that it may not allow anyone to perform righteous acts for God. That evil spirit wrestles against those who wish to become faithful. If some of those with this intent are praised as faithful, or as long-suffering, or as merciful, that evil spirit immediately wrestles against them. And it does vanquish some and their fruit is scattered and dies. It accustoms them to conduct their lives with mixed motives pleasing others. And so it destroys their fruit, though other people may imagine that they have fruit. In the presence of God, though, they have nothing. Because of this, God did not give them power. Instead, he sent them away empty,[3] since he did not find that their fruit is good, and he deprived them of the great sweetness of grace.

3. See Luke 1:53.

Letter 7

FROM THE SAME

Beloved in the Lord, I greet you in the spirit of gentleness, which is peaceful, which breathes a sweet fragrance upon the spirits of the just. That spirit does not approach any soul except those which have been completely purified from their own "old selves."[1] For it is holy, and cannot enter an impure soul.

In any case, our Lord did not give [this spirit] to his apostles until they had purified themselves. Because of this, he said to them that, "If I go away, I will send the Paraclete to you, the spirit of truth, and it will tell you all things."[2] This spirit gives itself to the souls of the just, from Abel and Enoch until today, to those souls which completely purified themselves. The spirit which approaches other souls is not this spirit, but the spirit of repentance. The spirit of repentance comes to other souls since it calls them all and washes them from their impurity. And when it has cleansed them completely, it gives them to the Holy Spirit, and does not cease pouring fragrance and sweetness upon them, just as Levi says, "And who knows the enjoyment of the spirit except those in whom it has made its home?"[3]

1. See Rom 6:6; Col 3:9.
2. John 16:7, 13. Paraphrase combining John 14:26; 15:26; 16:7.
3. Source unknown.

While many were held worthy of the spirit of repentance, the spirit of truth dwells in hardly any souls, from one generation to the next. Just like the pearl of great price, it is not found except in the souls of the just, those who have been made perfect. When Levi was found worthy of it, he gave a great prayer to God saying, "I sing to you, O God, because you favored me with the spirit which you gave to your servants."[4] Likewise, all the just to whom it was sent gave great thanks to God. This is the pearl which the gospel describes, which the man sold all his possessions to buy.[5] This, too, is the treasure, hidden in a field. When the man found it, he rejoiced greatly.[6] [The spirit] will dwell in these souls, will reveal a great mystery, and the night is as the day to them.[7] See, I have made known to you the working of this spirit.

You know that trials are not imposed on anyone, unless he has received the spirit. But when he has received the spirit, he is handed over to the devil to be tried. And who hands him over to [the devil]? The Spirit of God. For it is not possible for the devil to put a faithful one to trial, unless God first handed him or her over.

When your Lord was baptized, the Spirit brought him into the desert to be tried by the devil, and the devil could do nothing to him. But after these trials, the power of the Spirit adds new [spiritual] maturity to the holy ones, and a greater power.

So in all things let us praise the Lord, to whom let us also give thanks, whether we are in honor or in dishonor,[8] because he led us up from that murky air[9] and restored [us] to our former height.

---

4. Source unknown.
5. See Matt 13:45-46.
6. See Matt 13:44.
7. See Rev 21:25; Ps 138:12.
8. Rom 9:21; 2 Tim 2:20.
9. An echo of Psalm 17:12, though the import differs.

Letter 8

The wind blows where it wills.[1] It blows into bright, shining, divine souls, those yearning to serve [the Spirit] with all zeal. And if they obey the Spirit which is worthy of worship, it gives them fear of God, and fervor in the beginning. And when these things are present in them, it makes them hate the whole world and every harmful object of desire in it, whether gold or silver or some deceptive adornment for the body, or father, or mother, or wife and children.[2] It makes the work of God in them sweeter than honey and the honeycomb,[3] whether it is the toil of fasting or of vigils, or silence and service, or alms. It makes all that belongs to God sweet to them.

And when the Spirit teaches them all these things, it gives them over to be tested. And from then on, everything that was sweet to them becomes oppressive and irksome. Many who are inexperienced when they are tested remain in oppression and become carnal. These are those about whom Paul says, "Having begun with the spirit, do you now end with the flesh? Have you suffered such things in vain?"[4] "In vain," that is to say, that the one who endures labors on account of God and then completely sinks

---

1. John 3:8. "Wind" and "spirit" both translate the word πνεῦμα (*pneuma*).
2. See Matt 10:47.
3. Ps 18:11, etc.
4. Gal 3:3.

beneath their weight and does not call upon them[5] to help him not only loses the profit of these labors, but also becomes liable to heavier chastisement, having disdained and not having chosen the power from on high.

But if one withstands Satan in the first trial, and wins out over him, then God grants a fervor which is steady, quiet, and calm. The first fervor is uncertain, wavering and unsettled. But the second is better, and it gives birth to clear vision, producing perseverance, being calm and faithful and unambivalent. Like a ship in a calm harbor, having its two sails slackened, so the second fervor is restful in every way.

And so now, my beloved children, let us acquire the second fervor for ourselves, so that you may be eased in everything. For the fervor which concerns God cuts off all passion, and casts all dullness out of a person and makes the divine dwell with him, so that he becomes the temple of God according to the scripture, "I will dwell in them and walk among them."[6]

If you want the fervor which is absent to return to you, this is the task [required]: that one should make a covenant between himself and God, and say before [God], "Forgive me in what I have done in carelessness and I will no longer disobey you." Let him now be on guard from all carelessness, and not give himself a single rest of body or soul, but make his thoughts concentrated before God night and day, and at every hour he should cry in the presence of God, and chastened, reproach his own soul, [saying], "How have you been neglectful until today, left dry and barren all these days?" And so that he might remember the chastisement and the eternal kingdom, he should reproach himself every hour saying, "How God has blessed you with all these honors, and have you been neglectful? He has subjected every creature to you, and have you not rejected [the responsibility]?" And whenever he says

5. "Them," that is, the labors, that when accepted in the fear of God as coming from the Spirit are for the profit of the person.
6. 2 Cor 6:16.

these things in his soul, reproaching it night and day and every hour, at once the fervor of God comes to him, which is better in every way than the first.

When the blessed David saw the oppression that had come upon him he said, "I considered the days of old, and remembered the years long past, and I meditated,"[7] and again, "I remembered the days long past, I meditated on all your works. I was meditating on the creations of your hands. I stretched out my hands to you. My soul was as a waterless land to you."[8] And when you have been turned back, give yourself to the contemplation of the wonders of God. Then you will be saved,[9] by the grace of the Father and the Son and the Holy Spirit forever, amen.

7. Ps 76:6.
8. Ps 142:5-6.
9. See Isa 30:15 (Septuagint).

INSTRUCTIONS OF ABBA AMMONAS

The *Instructions* offer an example of the discourses of Abba Ammonas. Because they center on a single topic, in this case the four things that prevent repentance, this example provides evidence for the systematization of teaching among the monks in Abba Ammonas' monastic network. We may contrast this genre with the collection of detached sayings (*To Novices*) that follows, and with the two *Fragments*.

B.M.Z.

From the *Instructions*
of our Holy Father Ammonas [Four Teachings]

There are four things, and, if anyone has even one of them, that person cannot be converted, nor does God accept his prayer.

The first is arrogance. When people believe that they are living well, and that their conduct is pleasing both to God and to others, and that many are edified by meeting them, and that they escaped the mass of sins when they withdrew into the desert, if people believe these things, then God does not live with them. Rather, a monk must judge himself above the irrational beasts and hold that his work is not pleasing to God. It is said through the prophet that "all the righteous deeds of people are as polluted rags before his face."[1] And unless the soul is completely convinced of the truth that it is more impure even than the irrational beasts, than the birds, than dogs, God will not accept its prayer. For the irrational beasts, and the dogs, and the birds never sinned before God, nor do they come to judgment. From this it is clear that people are sinners more to be pitied than animals, for they would be better off to be like the beasts, neither being raised from the dead nor brought to judgment. Irrational beasts do not slander, and they are not arrogant, but they still love those who nurture them. But human beings do not love God as they should, although he formed and nurtures them.

The second is this—if anyone has a resentment against anyone else whomever and even if he blinded his own eyes against this person and still resents him, his prayer will not go up to God. Nor should such a

1. Isa 64:6.

one deceive himself that he has a portion of mercy or forgiveness from God, even if he should raise the dead.

Third, if someone judges a person who is sinning, he too is being judged, even if he should perform signs and wonders.[2] For Christ says, "Do not judge and you will not be judged."[3] For a Christian should not judge people, "for neither does the Father judge anyone, but has given all judgment to the Son."[4] So, anyone judging before Christ is an antichrist. Many who today are robbers and fornicators, tomorrow become holy and just,[5] and while we knew their sins, we did not perceive their hidden virtues, and we judged unfairly.

The fourth is—if anyone does not have love. For "apart from this," as the apostle says, "even if we speak with the tongues of angels, and we have all true faith, and we move mountains, and if we give whatever we have to the poor, and give our bodies over to martyrdom, it does not help us."[6] But perhaps you will say, "And how is it possible to give everything we have to the poor and not have love, since mercy is love?" But mercy is not complete love, but rather a part of love. Many give alms to some, while treating others unjustly, some they treat with hospitality, others with resentment, some they shelter, others they revile, they feel sympathy for strangers, but hate those closest to them. In short, this is not love, it is not, for love hates no one, reviles no one, judges no one, grieves no one.[7] It is disgusted at no one, neither the faithful nor the unfaithful, nor the stranger, nor the sinner, nor the fornicator, nor the unclean, but rather loves the sinners, the weak and the careless, and works on their behalf. It grieves and weeps [for them], and feels sympathy for the wicked even more than for the good. It imitates Christ, who called sinners, eating and drinking with them.[8] Because of this, to show what true love is, he taught saying, "Become good and merciful,

2. Matt 24:24, for example.
3. Matt 7:1.
4. John 5:22.
5. See *AP* 8 and 10; PG 65: 122-24; Ward, 23–24.
6. See 1 Cor 13:1-3.
7. See 1 Cor 13:4-7.
8. See Matt 9:11-13.

like your heavenly father, just as he sends rain upon the wicked and the good and makes the sun rise upon the just and the unjust."[9] So also the one who is truly loving loves all, has mercy on all, and prays for everyone. For there are some who practice works of mercy, and place their confidence in this alone, while committing many sins, and hating many, and defiling their bodies. These people deceive themselves, hoping in their works of mercy, which they believe they are doing.

9. See Matt 5:15.

About the Joy of the Soul of One Beginning to Serve God (To Novices)

1) Beloved brothers, let us fortify ourselves in tears before God. Perhaps his love will send an angel[1] to us, to guard us until we have made war, together with the [good deeds] we have done, against those rulers of evil which come against us.

2) Let us love living in peace with all, the little and the great. This peace will guard us from hatred when it comes out to meet us in battle. The one who is ill recognizes health. The one who is crowned is crowned because he has vanquished the enemies of the king. There is suffering, there also is virtue. But if we are careless, it is clear that we are like traitors.

3) A brave heart is an aid to the soul, after God, just as carelessness is an aid to evil.

4) This is the power of those wishing to possess virtue: if they fall, they will not be discouraged, but will once more take thoughtful care.

5) The tools of virtue are corporal works with understanding.

6) The fruits of the passions are born from carelessness.

7) Not judging one's neighbor is a wall for those fighting with understanding. To blame [a neighbor] destroys the wall in ignorance.

---

1. δύναμιν (*dynamin*)—literally "power."

8) Care of the tongue makes it clear that a person is practicing ascesis, but stupidity of tongue is a sign that a person does not possess virtue within.

9) Mercy with understanding gives birth to foresight and leads to love. But lack of mercy is a sign that there is no virtue in a person.

10) Goodness gives birth to chastity, but distraction gives birth to the passions. Hardheartedness gives birth to anger.

11) The asceticism of the soul is to hate distraction. The asceticism of the body is poverty.

12) To love distraction makes the soul fall away. The practice of stillness with understanding sets the soul upright.

13) An excess of sleep is a disturbance of the passions in the body. Keeping vigils in moderation is salvation to the heart. Much sleep coarsens the heart, but a praiseworthy vigil renders it supple. Much sleep darkens the soul, but vigils in moderation illuminates it. A good sleep, in silence, with knowledge, is counted above keeping vigils with chatter.

14) Holy sorrow[2] chases away every evil disturbance. Not to wound the conscience of a neighbor gives birth to humility.

15) Praise from people gives birth to arrogance little by little. To love boasting chases away knowledge.

16) Control of the stomach humbles the passions, but desire for food easily awakens them.

17) Adornment of the body is the ruin of the soul, but provision for [the body], according to the fear of God, is good.

---

2. Πένθος (*penthos*) is an important monastic term. It refers to the experience of seeing oneself as one is, and being grief-stricken. The tears which result are considered very beneficial, cleansing, and reconciling. See the classic study by Irénée Hausherr, *Penthos: The Doctrine of Compunction in the Christian East*, CS 53 (Kalamazoo, MI: Cistercian Publications, 1982).

18) To heed the judgments of God gives birth to the fear of God in the soul, but to trample down the conscience expels the virtues from the heart.

19) The love which is in God cuts off captivity, but boldness awakens it.

20) To guard the mouth arouses intention toward God, if it is silent with knowledge, but much talk gives birth to restlessness and madness.

21) To surrender your will to your neighbor is a sign that the mind sees the virtues, but that your will should rule in dealing with your neighbor is a sign of ignorance.

22) Practice, with fear, guards the soul from the passions, but to carry on conversations about the world hides the virtues from it.

23) To love matter disturbs the mind and the soul, but the renunciation of matter renews the mind and the soul.

24) To remain silent rather than reveal one's thoughts[3] makes it clear that you seek the honour of the world and its shameful glory.[4] But the one who speaks openly and declares his thoughts to his fathers chases them out of himself.

25) Just as a house which has neither door nor window, and into which any serpent which wants to enters, so also is one who does his work but does not keep watch over it.

26) Just as rust eats away iron, so to is the praise of people, if the heart trusts it.

27) Humility is in the first place of all the virtues; gluttony is in the first place of all the passions.

---

3. "Thoughts" translates λογισμούς (*logismous*), a technical word in the desert tradition which usually refers to temptations. Evagrius categorized the "thoughts" into eight—gluttony, lust, etc.—which Gregory the Great a few centuries later transformed into the seven deadly sins.

4. See Phil 3:19

28) Love is the fulfillment of the virtues; to pronounce oneself righteous is the fulfillment of the passions.

29) Just as a worm which eats away wood destroys it, so too evil in the heart hides the soul from the virtues.

30) To cast the soul before God gives birth to [the ability] to endure insult undisturbed, and the tears [of the soul] are safe from all human honors.

31) Not to blame oneself leads to the loss of the ability to endure anger.

32) To mix one's own conversation with those of the world disturbs the heart and dishonors the one praying to God through lack of frankness.

33) To love the business of the world renders the soul dark, but to look at it with suspicion in everything brings knowledge.

34) To love toil is hatred against the passions, but laziness easily brings them on.

35) Do not give yourself to public affairs and your thoughts will be silent in you.

36) Do not rely on your own ability, and God will come to your aid.

37) Have no enmity against another, since your prayer will not be acceptable. Live in peace with everyone so that your prayer may be confident.

38) Guard your eyes and your heart will surely not see evil. The one who looks upon anyone at any time with pleasure ends in adultery.

39) Do not wish to hear that harm [has befallen] one who has aggrieved you, so that you will not take revenge upon him in your heart.

40) Guard your ears, so that you do not gather conflicts to yourself.

41) Work at your manual labor so that you may provide the poor with bread,[5] for idleness is death and the ruin of the heart.

---

5. Rather awkward in the Greek—literally, "so that a poor person may find your bread."

42) Continual prayer destroys captivity; to grow careless little by little is the mother of forgetfulness.

43) One who expects that death is near will not sin much; the one expecting to live for a long time will become entangled in many sins.

44) As to the one who has made himself ready to give an account to God for all his works, God takes care to purify him from every way of sin. The one who is contemptuous and says that he will get there first dwells among the wicked.

45) Each day, before you do any work whatsoever, remember where you are, and, when you depart from your body, where you must go away to, and each day you will not be negligent of your soul.

46) Consider the honor which all holy ones have obtained, and their zeal will draw you little by little. Think again too about the reproaches which sinners obtain, and you will guard yourself from evils.

47) Always keep the counsel of the fathers, and you will spend all your life in rest.

48) Take care if your reason pricks at you [because] your brother has a grievance against you, lest you be contemptuous toward him, but repent before him in a supplicating voice until you convince him. Watch lest you become hardened against your brother, for we all do violence from hatred.

49) If you live with brothers, do not order them about in every matter, but labour with them, so that you may not lose your fruit.

50) If the daimons trouble you about food and clothing and set on you the shame of great poverty, do not answer them at all, but entrust yourself to God with your whole heart and you will find rest.

51) Watch lest you disregard doing your liturgical offices, for they bring enlightenment to the soul.

52) If you performed good deeds, do not boast to yourself. If you performed many evil deeds, your heart should not be grieved immoderately,

but stand firm against your heart, so that you may no longer be persuaded by them, and you will be protected from pride, if you are wise.

53) If you are troubled by lust, afflict your body ceaselessly in humility before God, and do not allow your heart to be persuaded that your sins have been forgiven, and you will find peace.

54) If gluttony makes war against you in the desire for [various] foods, remember their foul smell, and you will find peace.

55) If gossip about a brother bothers you, remember that if you listen he will have cause to complain, but if you turn aside from opposing him, you will have peace also.[6]

56) If pride dominates you, remember that it destroys all your work and that there is no repentance for those persuaded by it, and you will find peace.

57) If contempt for your neighbour makes war against your heart, remember that because of this, God will deliver you into the hands of your enemies,[7] and you will find peace.

58) If the beauty of a body tugs at your heart, remember its foul odor when it dies, and you will find peace.

59) If you are embattled by the pleasure of [the company of] women, as being the most pleasing to you, think of where those who are already dead have gone, and you will find peace.

60) Discernment gathers and considers all these things. It makes good deeds prosper and renders the bad ineffective. Discernment cannot come, unless you do its work. First, regarding silence, silence gives birth to ascesis and weeping. Weeping gives birth to fear. Fear gives birth to humility and foresight. Foresight gives birth to love, and love makes

---

6. The Greek here seems compressed and is difficult to pin down. The meaning is plain, though—a monk should not let gossip influence his thoughts or actions toward another monk. See sentences 7, 39, 40, 48, and 57 for similar expressions of the same sentiment.

7. Jer 21:7; Ezek 39:23.

the soul free from sickness, untroubled by passion.[8] Then, after all these things, a person knows that he or she is not far from God.

61) Let the one wishing to come to these rewards of the virtues, then, be detached and apart from every human being, so that he does not judge another, and he will make himself ready for death. And as often as he prays, let him consider what it is which separates him from God, and he will render it ineffective. And he will hate this world, and the goodness of God will soon grace him with the virtues. Learn this: everyone who eats and drinks immoderately, or who loves anything of this world, neither comes to these [rewards], nor attains them, but loves himself.

62) I beg all wishing to offer repentance to God to guard themselves from indulgence in wine, for it enflames all the passions and chases the fear of God from the soul.

63) Only beg from God with all your strength that he send the fear of God to you, so that through the longing which is for God, he may destroy all the passions which are warring against your wretched soul and which want to separate it from God so as to take possession of it. Without doubt, this is the reason why the enemies fight with every device at their disposal when they wage war against a person.

64) Pay no mind to rest, brother, as long as you are in this earthly body. And certainly do not trust yourself when you have a period of respite from the passions in this life, because the crafty ones hold themselves in their malice in check for awhile, until a person relaxes the heart, thinking that he can rest, and all of a sudden they rush into the miserable soul, and capture it like a sparrow. And if they become masters of it, they humiliate it mercilessly with every sinful action. It is more difficult to be forgiven [for these] than for those which you started praying for.

---

8. ἀπαθῆ (*apathē*) is a familiar word in the desert literature. Related to the English "apathy," it carries none of its negative connotations. Passions were not "deep feelings," as the word has come to mean in English (I might have a "passion" for studying the desert fathers, for example, which is a fine thing). They were instead unruly desires. The passions in the desert tradition distracted and clouded the mind and soul, and to be free of them was the goal of ascesis.

65) Let us stand in the fear of God, and let us be on guard, perfecting our practice, guarding all the virtues, which impede the evil of our enemies, because the labours and the difficulties of this little life not only guard us from wickedness, but they also in turn prepare crowns for our souls before we leave the body.

66) Let us flee, then, O brothers, the world and all that is in it, so that we may inherit the good things of heaven. For the inheritance of this world is gold and silver and houses and clothing, and not only prepares us to sin, but also, when we depart we [must] leave them behind. But the inheritance of God is without limit. That which the eye has not seen, nor the ear heard, and which has not entered the heart of a person, this God made ready to those who heed him in this little time,[9] and to those who do not receive this [inheritance] fruitlessly, but through bread and water and clothes, which they share with those in need, and through love of neighbor and purity of the body from corruption, and not doing injury to their neighbor, and the possession of a heart free from evil, and [through] the remainder of his commands.

67) Those who guard these things will have rest, and people will respect them in this world and they will receive eternal joy when they go out from the body.

68) Those who do their own will in sin, and do not wish to repent but are distracted by pleasure—who perfect their wickedness through self-deception, and the coarse jesting of their words, and the clamour in their quarrels, and their lack of fear for the judgment of God, and their hard-heartedness toward the poor—and the rest of their faults—in this age the faces of such as these are filled with shame, and people will despise them, and when they go out from this world, reproach and shame will pave their way to Gehenna.

69) But God is able to strengthen us and deems us worthy to advance in his works, we who guard ourselves from every evil work, so that

9. See 1 Cor 2:9.

we may be saved in the hour of trial which is about to come upon the whole world.

70) For our Lord Jesus Christ will not delay,[10] but will come bringing retribution with him. The godless he will send to the eternal fire,[11] but he will share with his own the reward, and they will go in with him and they will rest in his kingdom forever.

71) So do not lose heart, brother, as you read these things every day. Perhaps we too will find mercy, among those whom Christ has found worthy.

72) Take care, beloved, to observe these commands which have been written down, so that you may be able to be saved with the holy ones who are faithful to the commands of our Lord Jesus Christ. If anyone reads these things and does not observe them, he is like the one who looked at his face in a mirror, and immediately forgot what he looked like.[12]

73) But if anyone reads these things and observes them, he is like the seed that was sown in good ground and bore fruit.[13] God can see to it that we are found among the heedful and observant, so that he may receive from us, too, sound fruit through his grace. For his are the power and the glory and the authority forever and ever. Amen.

10. Hab 2:3; Heb 10:37.
11. See Matt 25:41.
12. Jas 1:23-24.
13. See Matt 13:8.

AMMONAS TWO FRAGMENTS

Fragment 1

1) "No one can serve two masters,"[1] says the Lord. You cannot do the things of God and the things of the world. "You cannot serve both God and Mammon."[2] You either [serve] God for God, or the world for the world. If you are cowardly, do not go out to war, for you cannot be both cowardly and warlike. For it is written, "Let not the cowardly go out to war."[3] You cannot be both weak and brave. You cannot be precise and careless. Yearn either for the friendship of God, or the friendship of people. The one who loves the friendship of people distances himself from the friendship of God. For it is written, "Fight to the death for truth."[4] The one who cares for the truth heeds the law of God completely, and the one who heeds the law of God opposes those who trample the law of God.

2) It is not good to wish to please all people. For it is written, "Woe to you when all speak well of you."[5] The prophets died for the sake of truth while the false prophets said what was pleasing to people, and were loved. You who wish to speak out from the truth, see that you also die for its sake. Do not do that which pleases people nor be loved by them. For example, what I understood, I wrote accordingly. Do that which

---

1. Matt 6:24.
2. Matt 6:24.
3. See Deut 20:8.
4. Sir 4:28.
5. Luke 6:26.

gives you rest. This is what I think, that if you do what is pleasing to people, they will later despise your unfaithfulness. If you are zealots for the truth, even if they are somewhat annoyed by you, later they will admire and praise your inspired zeal.

3) Let us flee unprofitable pairings with people, welcoming solitude. Contact with those closest to us is harmful and destructive of a peaceful state. Just as those who are strong, having become infected with the plague, are sick through their whole [bodies], so too do people living indiscriminately with others share wholly in their vices. For what do those who are set apart still have in common with the world?

Fragment 2

[Ammonas] said again, Sitting in your cell, recollect your mind. Keep the day of your death before you. Then see the decay of your body. Reflect on this eventuality. Accept your labor, observe the vanity of this world. Exercise your virtuousness and eagerness, so that you may be able to remain constantly in the same desire for tranquility[6] and not tire. Remember, too, the condition of the souls in Hell. Consider their state: in such bitter silence, in such terrible sighing. [Consider] with how much fear and struggle, or with what apprehension they await unceasing pain, and incorporeal, endless tears. But also bring to mind the day of resurrection and your appearance before God. Imagine that awesome judgment. Bring to the forefront of your mind [the condition of] those sinners whose shame awaits them in the presence of God and of his Christ, and angels and archangels, and powers[7] and all people. And [consider] all their punishments, the eternal fire, the worm that does not die,[8] Tartarus,[9] the darkness which is over all these things,

---

6. ἡσυχία (*hesychia*), elsewhere translated as "silence" or "the practice of stillness."

7. See 1 Pet 3:22.

8. Mark 9:43-48; Isa 66:24.

9. See 2 Pet 2:4.

the gnashing of teeth,[10] the fears and the tortures. But consider too that which is stored up for the just, confidence with God the father, and his Christ, the angels and archangels,[11] and the powers[12] and the whole people, and [consider] the kingdom and its gifts, the joy and the rest.

Consider the memory of each of these [two alternatives]. Groan over the judgment of the sinners, weep, and grieve, imagine yourself in their form, fearing lest you yourself may be among them. But as for the good things laid up for the just, rejoice, be merry and glad. Be eager to estrange yourself from the former, and to enjoy the latter. See, whether you happen to be in your cell or somewhere outside, that you never cast away the thought of the memory of these things, so that through this you may escape harmful temptations.[13]

10. See Matt 8:12; 13:42; etc.
11. See 1 Thess 4:16.
12. See Eph 6:12.
13. λογισμούς (*logismous*); see p. 143, n. 3.

THE *EXHORTATIONS (OR PARAGRAPHS OF ENCOURAGEMENT)* OF ABBA AMMONAS

The *Exhortations* of Abba Ammonas are evidence of the activity of monastic practice, of the daily challenges and hardships that faced monastics in their quest, and of the hope and solace that might be obtained in the process. Like the early monastic rules of Ammonas' contemporaries, the *Exhortations* served as guides in practical matters relating to personal development and social interaction. For this reason, they afford access to Abba Ammonas' conception of spiritual formation.

B.M.Z.

THE EXHORTATIONS
(OR PARAGRAPHS OF ENCOURAGEMENT)

I. [Christ, the Monk's Model]

Keep yourself scrupulously, beloved, since [ὡς] you are of good courage and believe that our Lord Jesus, although he was God and possessed indescribable glory and majesty, became our model [τύπος], in order that we might follow in his footsteps [1 Pet 2:21]. He humbled himself greatly and exceedingly on our behalf by taking the form of a slave [Phil 2:7], and he thought lightly both of much mendicity and of shame. He bore up against many violent and disgraceful acts, and, as it is written, "He was led as a sheep to the slaughter, and as a lamb before its shearer is dumb, so he does not open his mouth. He bore his judgment in his humiliation [ἐν τῇ ταπεινώσει]" [Is 53:7-8], and consented to death by means of many wanton acts of violence on our account. In consequence, because of his commandment, we too, [in order to atone] for our sins, endure zealously if anyone at all, justly or unjustly, maltreats us or dishonors us or fails us [ὑστερῇ[1]] or rails at us [1 Pet 2:12] or flogs us even to death. Even as a sheep being led to the slaughter and as a dumb beast [Is 53:7], do not speak out at all, but rather, if you are able, pray; but if not, at least be utterly silent with much lowliness.

II. [Affliction and Disgrace Are Gains]

Keep yourself scrupulously, believing that the acts of wanton violence and the disgraces and the humiliations that happen because of the

---

1. See Mark 10:21 for this unusual use of *hustereō*.

Lord are a great gain and the salvation of your soul. And endure them with zeal and without confusion, reckoning, "I am worthy to suffer even more on account of my sins, and it is a great thing for me, that I am counted quite worthy to suffer and to endure anything for the sake of the Lord. For perhaps through many oppressions and disgraces, I may at least, in some way or other, become an imitator of the suffering [πάθους] of my God."[2] And as often as you remember those who have oppressed you, pray for all of them from the heart and truthfully as patrons who have given you great gains, and do not in the least degree count anything against anyone. But if anyone honors or praises you, be distressed, and pray to be kept from this load, and so from every affair that has glory and preeminence to the very least. Entreat God earnestly from the heart and truthfully to remove such things far away from you, reckoning, "I am unworthy and weak." And always search scrupulously for the humbler ways of life and modes of discipline, and in them initiate yourself mournfully and humbly and unpretentiously, as almost dead and a corpse to this world, and as the worst [ἐσχατώτερος] and most sinful of all. For these are great gains for your soul.

III. [Self-Abasement]

Keep yourself scrupulously. As a great death and destruction of your soul and eternal punishment so you shall hate and loathe all love of rule and love of glory. You shall hate and loathe the wanting of glories or honors or praises from human beings, and the calculating that you are something, or that you have achieved virtue, or that "I am better than another," or at least the equal of another. You shall hate and loathe every base desire and fleshly pleasure to the very least. You shall hate and loathe observing a person if there is no need, and touching another body if there is no necessity, or saying to someone, "Where is this?" if there is no need, or eating a little or the least bit, if there is no need,

---

2. Ammonas quotes St. Ignatius, *Epistle to the Romans* 6: *epitrepsate moi mimētēn eina: tou pathous tou theou mou.* (Lightfoot's text, part two, vol. 2, p. 220. See below note 10.)

in order that, since you are keeping yourself and making yourself safe this way in the least things, you may not fall into a grave matter, and may not be altogether tested, and may not, because you disdain little things, little by little fall.

IV. [Self-Knowledge]

Keep yourself scrupulously, in order that you may beg the forgiveness of your sins in reality, and seek the salvation of your soul and the kingdom of heaven in every way, and be devoted to this life [σπουδάζῃς³] with all your might, that in thought and word and deed, as well as in clothing and deportment, you may humiliate yourself and make yourself disreputable, as a dung-hill and earth and dust, and last of all and slave of all, and that you may in this way always from the heart and truthfully consider yourself worse than, and more sinful than, every Christian. And consider that you are far away from each virtue, and that, in comparison with a Christian, "I am earth and dust, and all my justice is like the rag of a menstruous woman [Is 64:5], and unless by great pity and grace I receive mercy from God, [I will be undone⁴], since I am the author [αἴτιος] of eternal punishment rather than of life. For if

---

3. See Derwas J. Chitty, *The Desert a City: An Introduction to the Study of Egyptian and Palestinian Monasticism under the Christian Empire* (Crestwood, NY: St. Vladimir's, 1966), 2–3, on the *spoudaioi*.

4. Filling in (what I take to be) an example of aposiopesis by supplying *luthēsomai*. See Herbert Weir Smyth, *Greek Grammar*, rev. Gordon M. Messing (Cambridge, MA: Harvard University Press, 1956; orig. pub. 1920), § 2352d; and F. Blass and A. Debrunner, *A Greek Grammar of the New Testament and Other Early Christian Literature*, trans. and ed. Robert W. Funk (Chicago: University of Chicago Press, 1961), § 482. The (transliterated) Greek is: *kai ei mē eleei pollōi kai chariti eleēthō para Theou, epei aitios eimi tēs aiōniou kolaseōs mallon ē tēs zōēs*. See the translations of Nau, 461: *et ce n'est que par une grande faveur et par grâce que je puis trouver miséricorde devant Dieu, lorsque je suis plus digne de la punition éternelle que de la vie*; and Gerardus Vossius (Gerrit Vos), *S. abbatis Ammonae, Capita paraenetica decem et novem*, in *Sancti patris Ephraem syri opera omnia . . . nunc recens latinitate donata* (Anvers, 1619), col. 383: *& nisi magna commiseratione ac gratia, misericordiam à Deo consecutus fuero, aeterno potius supplicio, quam vita dignus ero.*

he wishes to dispute with me, I do not dare to lift up my head, for I am full of dishonor." And so with a mournful and humiliated soul, expecting death from day to day, cry out earnestly to God to set your soul right with great pity, and to show pity to you, in order that thus you may perceive yourself growing weary with grief and groaning, so as never to be joyful and never to laugh, but that always your laughter may be turned into mourning and your joy into sorrow, and you may always go with a sad countenance, saying, "My soul is filled with mockery" [Ps 37:8].

V. [Rule of Life]

Keep yourself scrupulously. Consider yourself worse and more sinful than every Christian. Always keep your soul mournful, humiliated, and filled with many groans. Be always silent and do not speak. Reflect on eternal darkness and on those who are being condemned there and who are suffering pain there, even as you reckon yourself to belong to those people there rather than to life,[5] since you are liable to such great punishment. From this time forward, as long as it is the right time for repentance for deliverance from those fears and great punishments (since in thought you have already died and are there), exert yourself to grasp that unintermitting mourning and weeping beforehand, and that great sorrow and shame; and, according to the will of God, seek labors and toils of the soul and body for yourself, and unceasingly work at them on account of your sins. Only keep your body, as much as you can, laboring unceasingly at the works of your hands and at fastings

---

5. This clause *kai hōs tōn ekei sauton logizomenos mallon aition ē tēs zōēs* is difficult, for *aition*, "responsible for, guilty of," is not used of persons, yet *tōn ekei* must refer to the condemned in the previous clause. Also, it is hard to see how one can be "responsible for life" (*tēs zōēs*). The textual tradition of this section of the *Exhortations* reflects the difficulty. Nau's text follows D (Paris, Coislin 370, 10th cent.). However, B (Paris, Coislin 303, 10th cent.) omits *aition* where D has it, and places it between *hōs* and *tōn*. Moreover, both A (1911 edition, based on an 11th cent. ms. at Jerusalem) and E (Paris, Coislin 283, 11th cent.) omit *aition* entirely in this clause. In view of the textual tradition I have omitted *aition* from the translation of this clause. I would like to thank the Rev. Fr. Mark Scott, OCSO, and Dr. Nada Conic for help in arriving at this position.

and at many other humiliations by God's favor, fulfilling the saying, "He is last of all and slave of all" [Mark 9:35, 10:44]. On the other hand, keep your soul, as much as you can, always and unceasingly at meditation [μελέτῃ] of the Scriptures, and in the course of a little interval of meditation groan and pray earnestly, and in this way be, in your mind [κατὰ τὴν διάνοιαν[6]], like one unceasingly saying the offices in the assembly-hall [σύναξιν ποιῶν[7]], that the demons may not find a place to throw wicked considerations into your heart.

VI. [Our Presence before Christ]

Keep yourself scrupulously, since you believe that our Lord died and lived on our behalf, and bought [ἠγόρασεν] us with his blood, in order that we may no longer live for ourselves, but for the Lord, who died and was raised on our behalf—since you are of good courage and believe that you are always in the presence of his eyes, having died to a bad conscience [συνειδήσει] and having departed from this world, and since you remain and are always present before him.

VII. [Be as a Slave before the Lord]

Keep yourself scrupulously, in order that, as a slave who follows his master with fear and trembling and great lowliness, and does not remove himself from him, but is ready to comply with his will, so you, too—whether you are standing or sitting or are alone or with someone—train yourself always to be as in the presence of God with fear and great trembling, both in body and soul, in order that you may always keep your body and soul fearful and trembling. As much as you can, be pure in your thinking from sordid considerations and every censure [καταγνώσεως[8]], and, with all humility and mildness and regard for

---

6. See n. 10 below.

7. Taking G. W. H. Lampe, *A Patristic Greek Lexicon* (Oxford, 1961), s.v., B.3 and E, together with Chitty, 22, on the *synaxis*.

8. Lampe, s.v., B.3 and E.

others and discipline [ἐπιστήμης[9]] and great humiliation, stand in the presence of the one who examines you, and do not at all have the boldness to lift up your head on account of your sins.

VIII. [Absolute Obedience]

Keep yourself scrupulously, as one who remains in his presence and is always at hand to comply readily with his will, whether for life or for death or for whatever tribulation, with great zeal and faith, and as one who always expects great and terrible trials to come upon you, even to great and fearful tribulations and tortures and a terrible death.

IX. [Priority of God's Will]

Keep yourself scrupulously. If any troublesome business [πρᾶγμα] happens to you, whether in word or in deed or in your mind [κατὰ διάνοιαν[10]], do not at all seek your own will or repose, but seek the will of God scrupulously, and be anxious to accomplish this completely, whether it manifestly holds tribulation or death [ἐὰν θλῖψιν καὶ ἐὰν θάνατον[11]], for his commandment is eternal life [John 12:50].

X. [Every Act a Thanksgiving]

Keep yourself scrupulously. Since you are always in the presence of God, do nothing besides his purpose, but whether you wish to eat or

9. E. A. Sophocles, *Greek Lexicon of the Roman and Byzantine Periods (From B.C. 146 to A.D. 1100)*, Memorial Edition, corr. J. H. Thayer (Cambridge, MA: Harvard University Press, 1914; orig. pub. 1870), s.v.

10. See I Clement 19, where the phrase *kata dianoian* is translated "in our mind" by Bishop Lightfoot. See J. B. Lightfoot, *The Apostolic Fathers*, 2nd ed., part 1, vol. 2 (Peabody, MA: Hendrickson, 1989; orig. pub. 1889–90), 69 and 282. Reference to I Clem. in Walter Bauer, William F. Arndt, and F. Wilbur Gingrich, *A Greek-English Lexicon of the New Testament and Other Early Christian Literature* (Chicago: University of Chicago Press, 1957), s.v.

11. See Rom 14:8 (*ean te . . . ean te*), and Blass, Debrunner, and Funk, § 454 (3).

drink or go to sleep or visit someone or do any business whatever, first
test whether it is by the favor of God, and then so do it, as is fitting in
the presence of God, in order that this way in all your words and deeds
you may give a thanksgiving [ἐξομολόγησιν[12]], and through this have
a great attachment and diligence towards him.

XI. [Regard Yourself as an Unworthy Slave]

Keep yourself scrupulously, as one who knows that it is written,
"We are unprofitable slaves, we have done what we are bound to do"
[Lk 17:10]. If you ever do anything in your works by the favor of God,
do it not as for hire, but with all humility as in reality an unprofitable
slave and as one who is liable for much [πολλῶν χρεώστης]. And if you
do anything, consider yourself always as lacking much of what you
owe, and as adding to your sins almost every day through your negli-
gence. "For it is a sin for him who knows how to do good and does not
do it" [James 4:17]. And so far as you fall short of the commandments
of God, it is necessary that you always groan and beg God earnestly
and unceasingly to pardon you your sins with great pity and clemency
[φιλανθρωπίᾳ[13]], and to take pity on you.

XII. [If Injured, Make No Response while Angry]

Keep yourself scrupulously, in order that, if you are afflicted by any
troublesome business whatever, and pain or anger occurs in you, you
may be quiet and say nothing at all besides what is seemly, until your
heart is first made calm by unceasing prayer, and then you may thus
entreat your brother. If ever you must reprimand your brother, and you
see him in anger or confusion, say nothing to him, in order that he may
not be stirred up worse with anger; but if you see both yourself and
that brother in great composure and mildness, then at that time speak,
not as one who reprimands, but as one who is mindful with all humil-

---

12. Lampe, s.v. 3, where this passage is quoted.
13. Lampe, s.v.

ity and mildness that you not speak a word of your mouth in anger. Contend always as one who is of good courage and believes that you are in the presence of the eyes of God, and as one who sees him always. Tremble at him this way and fear him, knowing that in comparison with his indescribable glory and majesty you are as one who has no being [see Ps 103:33], as earth and dust [see Job 30:19], and rottenness and a worm [see Job 2:9c].

XIII. [One's Will Must Be Entirely Subject to God's]

Keep yourself scrupulously, since you believe that the Lord, although he was rich, died because of us [δι᾽ ἡμᾶς], and lived on our behalf [ὑπὲρ ἡμῶν], and bought us with his blood, in order that you too, because you were bought for a price, may no longer live for yourself, but for the Lord. Be his perfect slave in every respect, that you may perfect freedom from passions [ἀπάθειαν[14]] completely. And as a gentle beast is indisputably obedient to its master, so be always in God's presence, since you are perfectly dead to human passions and every pleasure, with no personal will or desire at all. But always keep your whole will and all your desire for working the will of God, in order that in this way you may never reckon that you are free or have your own power of choice [ἐξουσίαν], but that you may say, "I am God's slave, and it is necessary for me to comply with and follow his will." And keep yourself as one who expects temptation to come upon you every day—whether by [εἰς[15]] death or tribulation or great dangers—for you to bear readily and without being stirred up, considering that "through many tribulations it is necessary for us to enter the kingdom of heaven" [Acts 14:22].

XIV. [God's Will Greater than Human Wisdom]

Keep yourself scrupulously, as one who is always in God's presence, in order that, if any troublesome business happens to you, whether in

14. Lampe, s.v.
15. Sophocles, s.v. 4.

deed or in your mind, you may not at all seek your own will or repose. But always yearn after and accomplish the will of God scrupulously and perfectly, even if it manifestly involves trouble (but in reality contains the kingdom of heaven and the crown of life), believing with your whole heart that this is of advantage beyond all human wisdom, for the commandment of the Lord is eternal life [John 12:50], and those who love him "will not have less of every good" [Ps 33:11].

XV. [Make Every Act a Thanksgiving]

Keep yourself scrupulously. Since you are always in the presence of God, do nothing besides his purpose, but if you wish to do something, whether to work at or to say the least thing, or to visit or meet someone, or to go to sleep or do any other business whatever, first test whether this is a rational and needful business [χρεία εὔλογος] or the will of God; and so you will give thanks [ἐξομολογήσει¹⁶] in God's presence with great fear and trembling, that thus you may have a genuine relation and conversation with God. But give a thanksgiving both in all your words and in all your deeds. And if you lay a charge against yourself that you acted in transgression of these limits, strive to repent and to grieve with godly sorrow [λυπεῖσθαι¹⁷] and to pray to God to set you up straight, that you may not condemn [ἀνακρίνων¹⁸] yourself and perhaps make yourself fall.

XVI. [Place All Your Hope in God]

Keep yourself scrupulously, as one who is always in God's presence, in order that you may hope for nothing from anybody, except from him alone with faith. And if you have need, ask God that the thing you need may come to you according to his will. And always give thanks to God because of the things you find, since he has given them to you. And if

16. Lampe, s.v.
17. Lampe, s.v.
18. Lampe, s.v.

you fail to obtain something, since you do not hope at all in men, do not be aggrieved or mutter at all against anyone, but bear this earnestly and without confusion, considering, "I am worthy of many tribulations because of my sins—except if God wish to pity me, he is able both in a little time and in no time at all to fulfill all my need."

XVII. *[Accept Nothing Unless from God]*

Keep yourself scrupulously. Take and receive nothing, unless you are fully persuaded that God has given it to you. And receive what you see [comes[19]] from the fruit of justice both with all peace and love, but push away and throw aside such things as you see [come] from injustice with struggle and deceit and hypocrisy, considering that "better a small portion with fear of the Lord than many fruits [γεννήματα[20]] with injustice" [Prov 15:16, 29a].

XVIII. *[Silence One's Mode of Life]*

Keep scrupulously to yourself [κατὰ σαυτόν[21]], so that your great contest and exercise is always being silent and struggling not to speak at all the least little bit, even so far as saying to someone, "Where is this?" or, "What is that?" But if it ever becomes necessary for you to say something, first test by yourself whether it is a rational and needful business and the will of God, then speak, for this is superior to [ὑπέρ[22]] being silent. And accordingly confess to God the cause of the word which you wish to speak, and so finally, as one ministering to the will of God, open your mouth with the word of God, and speak whether short or long with all humility and mildness. And while you speak, keep [ἔχε] your countenance and your reasoning consistent with [μετά] a respectful and

---

19. Nau, 469–70, supplies "provenir" in brackets both here and below.

20. I take the liberty of reading *genēmata* for Nau's reading given above. See Bauer, Arndt, and Gingrich, s.v., and Rahlf's *Septuaginta*, ad loc.

21. Bauer, Arndt, and Gingrich, s.v. *kata* II.c.

22. Bauer, Arndt, and Gingrich, s.v.

deferential discourse. If you meet anyone, after you have said one or two words with love, be silent[23] beyond that, and if you are questioned closely about something of necessity, listen, and nothing more.

XIX. [Self-Control]

Keep yourself scrupulously, in order that, just as you abstain from fornication, so you may abstain also from the desire of the eyes [1 John 2:16], and from the sense of hearing, and from the mouth. On the one hand, keep your eyes fixed only on your work, not looking up except when there is a rational and needful business. On the other hand, do not at all observe a woman or a handsome man without great necessity. Do not agree to listen to reports against anyone, or to unprofitable talk, but always keep your mouth silent, in order that, since you are doing so, you may find mercy from the Lord God, to whom be glory and power forever and ever. Amen.

23. Nau places a comma after *hupopiptontos*, and takes *hopōs* as a final conjunction introducing a purpose clause. However, there should be a period following *hupopiptontos*, in my opinion, and *hopōs* with the aorist subjunctive *siōpēsēis* should be read as a command (see Liddell, Scott, and Jones, s.v. A.III.8).

Select Bibliography

Athanasius. *The Life of Antony*. Cistercian Studies Series 202. Translated and introduced by Tim Vivian and Apostolos N. Athanassakis. Kalamazoo, MI: Cistercian Publications, 2003.

Barnes, Timothy D. *Athanasius and Constantius*. Cambridge, MA: Harvard University Press, 1993.

Brakke, David. *Athanasius and the Politics of Asceticism*. New York: Oxford University Press, 1995.

Brown, Peter R. L. *The Body and Society: Men, Women, and Sexual Renunciation in Early Christianity*. New York: Columbia, 1988.

_____. *The Making of Late Antiquity*. Cambridge, MA: Harvard University Press, 1978.

Burton-Christie, Douglas. *The Word in the Desert: Scripture and the Quest for Holiness in Early Christian Monasticism*. New York: Oxford University Press, 1993.

Caner, Daniel. *Wandering, Begging Monks: Spiritual Authority and the Promotion of Monasticism in Late Antiquity*. Berkeley and Los Angeles: University of California Press, 2002.

Cayre, Fulbert. *Spiritual Writers of the Early Church*. Translated from the French by W. Webster Wilson. New York: Hawthorn, 1959.

Chitty, Derwas J. *The Desert a City: An Introduction to the Study of Egyptian and Palestinian Monasticism under the Christian Empire*. Oxford: Blackwell, 1966.

_____, ed. and trans. *The Letters of Ammonas: Successor of St. Antony*. Revised with introduction by Sebastian Brock. Oxford: SLG Press, 1979.

_____, ed. *The Letters of St. Antony the Great*. Oxford: SLG Press, 1975.

Clark, Elizabeth A. *Reading Renunciation: Asceticism and Scripture in Early Christianity*. Princeton, NJ: Princeton University Press, 1999.

Drijvers, Hans J. W. "Hellenistic and Oriental Origins." In *The Byzantine Saint* by Sergei Hackel, 25–33. San Bernardino, CA: The Borgo Press, 1983.

Ferguson, Everett. *Backgrounds of Early Christianity*. 3rd ed. Grand Rapids, MI: Eerdmans, 2003.

Goehring, James E. "Monastic Diversity and Ideological Boundaries in Fourth-Century Christian Egypt." *Journal for Early Christian Studies* 5, no. 1 (1997): 61–83. This article was republished in his work *Ascetics, Society and the Desert: Studies in Early Egyptian Monasticism*. Harrisburg: Trinity Press International, 1999.

Golitzin, Hieromonk Alexander. "'Earthly Angels and Heavenly Men': The Old Testament Pseudepigrapha, Nicetas Stethatos, and the Tradition of 'Interiorized Apocalyptic' in Eastern Christian Ascetical and Mystical Literature." *Dumbarton Oaks Papers* 55 (2001): 125–53.

Gould, Graham. *The Desert Fathers on Monastic Community*. New York: Oxford University Press, 1993.

Harmless, William. *Desert Christians: An Introduction to the Literature of Early Monasticism*. New York: Oxford University Press, 2004.

Judge, Edwin A. "The Earliest Use of Monachos for 'Monk' and the Origins of Monasticism," *Jahrbuch für Antike und Christentum* 20 (1977): 72–89.

Kirschner, Robert. "The Vocation of Holiness in Late Antiquity." *Vigiliae Christianae* 38 (1984): 105–24.

Klejna, Franz. "Antonius und Ammonas: Eine Untersuchung uber Herkunft und Eingenart der Altesten Monchsbriefe." *Zeitschrift für katholischen Theologie* 62 (1938): 309–48.

Kmosko, Michael. "Ammonii eremitae epistulae." *Patrologia Orientalis* 10 (1914).

Leinhard, Joseph. "'Discernment of Spirits' in the Early Church," *Theological Studies* 41 (1980): 505–29.

Louth, Andrew. *Origins of the Christian Mystical Tradition: From Plato to Denys*. Oxford: Clarendon, 1981.

Malherbe, Abraham J. *Moral Exhortation: A Greco-Roman Sourcebook*. Philadelphia: Westminster, 1986.

Nau, F. "Ammonas, successeur de Saint Antoine," *Patrologia Orientalis* 11 (1915).

Outtier, B., with A. Louf, M. Van Parys, Cl.-A. Zirnheld. *Lettres des Peres du Desert: Ammonas, Macaire, Arsene, Serapion de Thmuis*. Translated with introduction and notes. Begrolles-en-Mauges, 1985.

Rapp, Claudia. "'For Next to God, You Are My Salvation': Reflections on the Rise of the Holy Man in Late Antiquity." In *The Cult of Saints in Late Antiquity and the Middle Ages: Essays on the Contribution of Peter Brown*, edited by James Howard-Johnston and Paul Antony Hayward, 63–82. Oxford University Press, 1999.

Rousseau, Philip. *Ascetics, Authority, and the Church in the Age of Jerome and Cassian*. New York: Oxford University Press, 1978.

_____. "Ascetics as Mediators and as Teachers." In *The Cult of Saints in Late Antiquity and the Middle Ages: Essays on the Contribution of Peter Brown*, edited by James Howard-Johnston and Paul Antony Hayward, 45–62. Oxford University Press, 1999.

_____. "Christian Asceticism and the Early Monks." In *Early Christianity: Origins and Evolution to AD 600*, edited by Ian Hazlett. Nashville, TN: Abingdon Press, 1991.

Rubenson, Samuel. "Christian Asceticism and the Emergence of the Monastic Tradition." In *Asceticism*, edited by Vincent Wimbush and Richard Valantasis. New York: Oxford University Press, 1995.

———. *The Letters of Antony*. Minneapolis: Fortress Press, 1995.

Spidlik, Tomas. *The Spirituality of the Christian East: A Systematic Handbook*. Cistercian Studies Series 79. Translated by Antony P. Gythiel. Kalamazoo, MI: Cistercian Publications, 1986.

Stewart, Columba. *"Working the Earth of the Heart": The Messalian Controversy in History, Texts, and Language to AD 431*. New York: Oxford University Press, 1991.

Stowers, Stanley K. *Letter Writing in Greco-Roman Antiquity*. Philadelphia: Westminster, 1986.

Swan, Laura. *The Forgotten Desert Mothers: Sayings, Lives, and Stories of Early Christian Women*. New York: Paulist Press, 2001.

Valantasis, Richard. *Spiritual Guides of the Third Century: A Semiotic Study of the Guide-Disciple Relationship in Christianity, Neoplatonism, Hermetism, and Gnosticism*. Minneapolis: Fortress Press, 1991.

Veilleux, Armand, trans. *Pachomian Koinonia*. 3 vols. Kalamazoo, MI: Cistercian Publications, 1980–81.

Vivian, Tim. "The Good God, the Holy Power, and the Paraclete: 'To the Sons of God' (*Ad filios Dei*) by Saint Macarius the Great." *Anglican Theological Review* 30, no. 3 (1988): 338–65.

von Hertling, Ludwig. "Antonius der Einsiedler." In *Forshungen z. Geschichte d. innerkirchliche Leben* I, 56–60.

Ward, Benedicta, trans. *The Sayings of the Desert Fathers*. Cistercian Studies Series 59. Kalamazoo, MI: Cistercian Publications, 1975.

Wilken, Robert Louis. *The Spirit of Early Christian Thought: Seeking the Face of God*. New Haven, CT: Yale University Press, 2003.